Lakȟótiya Wóglaka Po!
Speak Lakota!

2

Level 2 Lakota Language Textbook

Lakota Language Consortium

Note: This is a dual teacher/student Lakota language textbook. It is designed to be used in conjunction with the Level 2 Audio CD's and the Level 2 Flashcard supplement pack. It is also intended to be used as a continuation of the Level 1 textbook and flashcards.

Lakota Language Consortium, Inc., Bloomington, Indiana 47408
© 2005 by Lakota Language Consortium Inc.
All rights reserved. Published 2005
Second Printing

ISBN: 0-9761082-5-9

Author: Jan Ullrich
Illustrations: František Valer
Layout: Jan Ullrich

The Lakota Language Consortium is a 501(c)3 tax-exempt nonprofit organization. Contributions are greatly appreciated and tax-deductible to the fullest extent of the law. Contact us at **contribute@lakhota.org** for more information.

Visit us at: **www.lakhota.org**
Textbook-related questions or comments may be sent to the author: **jfu@lakhota.org** (or jfu@centrum.cz).

Printed in Singapore

Native Consultants and Reviewers

There were many prominent native Lakota speakers, elders and educators who reviewed and consulted on this textbook. They all gave encouraging comments and positive assessments of the overall textbook structure, linguistic and cultural content and recommended it to be used to teach Lakota language in schools.

Consultants and reviewers from the Pine Ridge Indian Reservation:

John Around Him, Kayo Bad Heart Bull, Tim Bad Hart Bull, Irma Bad Wound, Elmer Bear Eagle, Wade Broken Nose, Darlene Last Horse, Randy Lays Bad, Gary Lays Bad, Darrel Lays Bad, Arlette Loud Hawk, Leonard Little Finger, Phinette Little White Man, Elisabeth Makes Him First, Leola One Feather, Mary Ann Red Cloud, Verola Spider, Edward Starr, Ivan Starr, Fred Stands, Sylvia Tobacco, Sam Two Bulls, Clarence Wolf Guts, John Yellow Hawk, Russell Yellow Thunder, Dennis Yellow Thunder

Consultants and reviewers from the Cheyenne River Indian Reservation:

Vivian High Elk, Suela High Elk, Matthew Iron Hawk, Harry Little Thunder, Arvol Looking Horse, Matthew Uses The Knife, Dave West

Consultants and reviewers from the Rosebud Indian Reservation:

Dinah Crow Dog, Sam High Crane, Steve Emery, Ira High Pipe, Robert Left Hand Bull, Ann Mae Bull Eagle, Darrel Standing Elk, Marianne Walking Eagle

Consultants and reviewers from the Standing Rock Indian Reservation:

Victor Brave Thunder, Joan Chief Eagle, Helmina Makes Him First, Delores Taken Alive, Dana Yellow Fat

Lakota Language Consortium makes every effort to involve fluent speakers in developing and reviewing these textbooks. In this way, local dialectical variations are represented from every major Lakota reservation. The textbooks utilize the prevailing words or phrases and include all other variations in the teacher's guide section.

Acknowledgments

This book would not be possible without the assistance and determination of many people along the way. We would like to acknowledge our gratitude and appreciation to these people and organizations for helping in a variety of ways to make this book possible:

John Around Him, Kayo Bad Heart Bull, Tim Bad Heart Bull, Sidney Bad Moccasin, Elmer Bear Eagle, Evelyn Black Moon, Mark Bordeaux, Robert Brave Heart, Victor Brave Thunder, Richard Broken Nose, Wade Broken Nose, Clifford Canku, Tom Casey, John Cedar Face, Bryan Charging Cloud, Joan Chief Eagle, Konstantin Chmelnicky, Cornelius Conroy, Steve Dubray, Less Duchenaux, Iris Dupris, Ben Eagle Elk, Steve Emery, Cecilia Fire Thunder, Mary Fire Thunder, Melvin Grey Owl, Carol Ann Heart, Arlee High Elk, Betty High Elk, Suela High Elk, Vivian High Elk, Bryant High Horse, Reva High Horse, Peter Hill, Bernadette Hollow Horn, Fern Hollow Horn, Johnson Holy Rock, Twila Hopkins, Matthew Iron Hawk, Mannie Iron Hawk, Lyle Jack, Calvin Jumping Bull, Felix Kidder, Philomine Lakota, Lenka Ullrichová, Darlene Last Horse, Darrell Lays Bad, Gary Lays Bad, James Lays Bad, Shaina Lays Bad, Randy Lays Bad, Leonard Little Finger, Harry Little Thunder, Aloysius Little White Man, Phinette Little White Man, Kevin Locke, Arlette Loud Hawk, Russell Loud Hawk, Arvol Looking Horse, Ivan Looking Horse, Heike Meya, Wilhelm Meya, Elisabeth Makes Him First, Helmina Makes Him First, Wilmer Mesteth, Amanda Morrisette, the Oglala Sioux Tribe, Gerald One Feather, Ingrid One Feather, Leola One Feather, Emanuel Red Bear, Mary Ann Red Cloud, Pat Red Elk, Gary Richards, David Rood, Alvin Slow Bear, Steve Slow Bear, Verola Spider, Darrel Standing Elk, Fred Stands, Edward Starr, Ivan Starr, John Steele, Petr Škaroupka, Delores Taken Alive, Jesse Taken Alive, Virgil Taken Alive, Babette Thin Elk, Chubbs Thunder Hawk, Sylvia Tobacco, Feleta Two Bulls, Sam Two Bulls, Robert Two Crow, Rick Two Dogs, Matthew Uses the Knife, Alex White Plume, Clarence Wolf Guts, John Yellow Hawk, James Yellow Horse, Amelia Yellow Thunder, Dennis Yellow Thunder, Russell Yellow Thunder and all the other people that have helped and supported this project along the way. *Wóphila tȟáŋka.*

The author would like to express special thanks to the following people: Leonard Little Finger, Richard Broken Nose, Johnson Holy Rock, Wil Meya and David Rood, for their commitment and hard work on behalf of the Lakota language revitalization; Steve Emery and Alex White Plume for major support of the Lakota Language Consortium; Gerda Brunner and Nina Webster for generously supporting the development of this textbook in numerous ways, their help has been invaluable; David Konvičný for donating his time to supporting the computers for the project; Jess Latham for donating the Lakota version of his Print Clearly and Print Clearly Dashed fonts; To "People of the Rainbow" from Slovakia; to Michal Pelíšek, Petra Pelíšková, Dušan Hanák, Petra Hanáková, Luděk Rektořík, Soňa Kryštofová, Pavel Černý, Xenie Rajnochová, Inka Křížová and many others from the Czech Republic for making small but important contributions.

The generosity of the following people made publication of this textbook possible: Dr. Eric Brewer Ph.D., Gerda Brunner, Helen Denton, Darrel Hallbick, James T. Hamilton, Barbara Lindgren, Nancy MacMahon, Kent McCurdy, Sioux Chief Manufacturing Company, Mark Warren, Washington Redskins Charitable Foundation, Jennifer Weaver, Nina Webster, and Laura Weyers.

The Lakota Language Consortium would also like to especially thank: **James P. Brown** of Bemidji, Minnesota; Peter Hinz-Rosin; Dirk Rohrbach; and the **Tatanka Oyate Verein zur Unterstützung indigener Völker e.V** of Germany, for their generosity and dedication to restoring the Lakota language. **Líla Wóphila Tȟaŋka!**

TATANKA OYATE
Verein zur Unterstützung indigener Völker e.V.

Table of Contents

Introduction

Dear Lakota educator and parent,

As Lakota people, we have endured many hardships over the years. Yet despite the suffering, our traditions, our history, our identity, and our religion have lived on. Our ways have been passed down to us for thousands of generations. Language is one of the most important of these. It embodies our prayers, our songs, our stories, and our ways. Lakota is a beautiful and sacred language that allows us to be who we are and connects us to our ancestors. We need it to be truly Lakota. It lets us speak from the heart in the old ways.

Today, however, our language is in grave danger and very little time remains to rescue it. Your grandchildren and great-grandchildren need your help for it to survive. As teachers and parents, the continuation of our language rests in your hands. If not enough children are taught to speak Lakota, the language will die. Without your help, our language will cease to exist in a spoken form in the near future. Your work is essential to raising a new generation of Lakota speakers before this happens.

There are many things that can be done to help stop the loss of our language. Some of the most important are to use the language in the home and to create language proficiency and literacy in the schools. You can have an important role in making this happen. Through hard work and commitment to the language, it is possible to promote a new age group of Lakota speakers who will eventually raise their own children speaking Lakota. This must be the ultimate goal of all our work.

This textbook series is designed to help you teach children to become Lakota speakers using proven language-learning methods; those that imitate natural language learning. With consistent and correct use of these materials, the average student should be able to achieve Lakota language proficiency after four years and fluency several years thereafter. The Level 1 textbook is designed in conjunction with the Level 1 Flashcard set and uses TPR methods to contextualize and internalize the vocabulary. This Level 2 textbook will help you reinforce this vocabulary and help you teach Lakota reading and writing. Ideally, the textbooks should be used three to four times a week for 30-40 minutes to achieve maximum results. Textbook instruction can also be augmented with visual aids, alphabet strips, posters, and picture books. We encourage you to utilize the Lakota Fonts used in these textbooks and a Lakota MSWord compatible spell checker to create your own worksheets and assessment materials. You should also regularly check **www.lakhota.org** for updates, tests, and additional exercises.

In addition to the textbooks, we also highly recommend that you attend at least one teacher-training workshop. These trainings have been greatly appreciated by the teachers who have completed them. They can be arranged most times throughout the year.

All these tools are made available to assist you in language instruction in the home and in the classroom. A great deal of work has gone into making these materials the highest quality possible in the hope that you may have all resources necessary for language preservation. Over forty-five Lakota elders and educators from all the major reservations as well as leading Lakota-language linguists have reviewed and developed these materials. Much effort was put into making the books reflective of community dialects and perspectives.

But books alone cannot save our language. Preserving Lakota depends on individual people making the decision to use or to teach Lakota to the best of their abilities. As a teacher and parent, you have a distinctive role in saving our language and making it special for *uŋkítȟakóžapi*. We hope you and your children enjoy these textbooks and that they become a memorable experience on the road to fluency. *Čhaŋtéwašteya napéčhiyuzape ló.*

Yours Sincerely,

The Board of Directors

Lakota Language Consortium

Lakota alphabet

A
agúyapi

Aŋ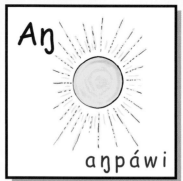
aŋpáwi

B
bébela

G
gnaška

Ǧ
ǧí

H
hokšíla

Ȟ
ȟé

KȞ
kȟáŋta

K'
k'á

L
lowáŋ

M
matȟó

PȞ
pȟahíŋ

P'
p'ó

S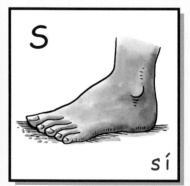
sí

Š
šúŋka

Lakȟóta oówaptaya slolwáye kštó.

U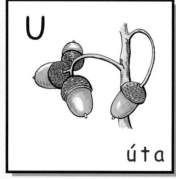
úta

Uŋ
uŋčí

W
wičhíŋčala

OÓWAPTAYA

Č
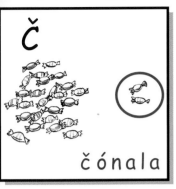
čónala

ČH
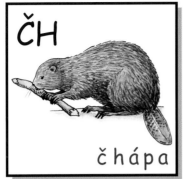
čhápa

Č'

č'ó

E
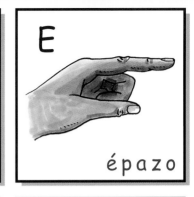
épazo

I

igmú

Iŋ

íŋyaŋ

K

kimímela

KH

khéya

N
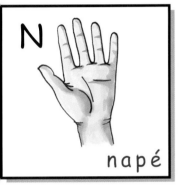
napé

O

oákaŋke

P

pispíza

PH
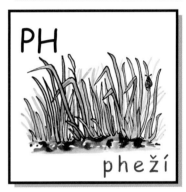
pheží

T
4
tópa

TH

thípi

TȞ

tȟatȟáŋka

T'
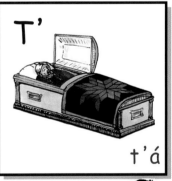
t'á

Y
3
yámni

Z

zičá

Ž

žó

I know the Lakota alphabet.

ix

1 Tuktél yathí hwo/he?   Where do you live?

1 What are their names?

Táku eníčiyapi he?

Bob emáčiyapi.

Lisa emáčiyapi.

Hello, my name is Bob and I am from Pine Ridge. My cousin and I are learning Lakota from our grandfather. We like speaking Lakota. Come speak Lakota with us! Lakȟótiya wóglaka po!

Hello, my name is Lisa. I am from Rosebud. I have been learning Lakota from my mother. My cousin Bob and I would like to help you learn Lakota too. It is fun.

Let's have a good time going through this book together. There are lots of fun ways to learn Lakota in it. We'll show you how to say Lakota words and sentences.

Saying your name.

Listen to and read Bob and Lisa's dialog. Can you guess what they are saying? Try to answer the following questions:

1. What do boys say at the end of a question? _____

2. What do girls say at the end of a question? _____

3. How do you say **"What is your name?"** in Lakota?

_____

4. How do we say **"My name is _____."** in Lakota?

_____

3 Reading and writing Lakota oral vowels.

Aa

aǧúyapi

a a a

A A A

Ee

épazo

e e e

E E E

Ii

igmú

i i i

I I I

Oo

oákaŋke

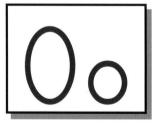

o o o

O O O

Uu

úta

u u u

U U U

4 🔊 Listen and fill in the proper vowel

| a | e | i | o | u |

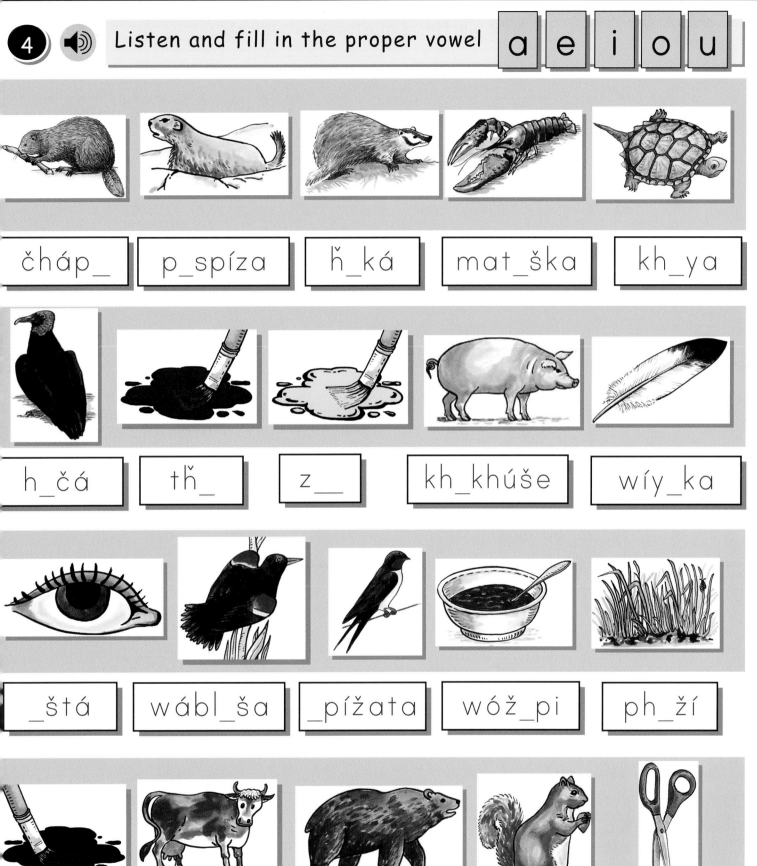

čháp_   p_spíza   ȟ_ká   mat_ška   kh_ya

h_čá   tȟ_   z__   kh_khúše   wíy_ka

_štá   wábl_ša   _pížata   wóž_pi   ph_ží

sáp__   pt_gléška   matȟ_   z_čá   wíy_kse

⑤ 🔊 Reading and writing Lakota nasal vowels.

Aŋ aŋ

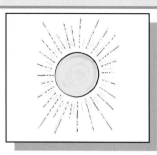

aŋpáwi

aŋ aŋ aŋ

Aŋ Aŋ Aŋ

Iŋ iŋ

íŋyaŋ

iŋ iŋ iŋ

Iŋ Iŋ Iŋ

Uŋ uŋ

uŋčí

uŋ uŋ uŋ

Uŋ Uŋ Uŋ

6 🔊 Listen and fill in the proper nasal vowel aŋ iŋ uŋ

w___blí   ___yaŋ   ___čí   čh____

s_____   š__ka   itȟ__kala   s__téȟla

1

čh___pȟá   h__háŋ   w__ží   pȟah__   h_yákȟuŋ

w__yaŋ   ___zóǧe   š__gmánitu   h__pa   s_kpȟé

7 Read and listen to the dialog. Where do they live? What is the Lakota name for each oyáŋke?

Háu, Tom emáčiyapi.
Íŋyaŋ Woslál Háŋ él wathí.
Tuktél yathí hwo?

Háŋ, Betty emáčiyapi.
Wakpá Wašté él wathí.

Lakȟóta Makȟóčhe

Sisseton

Standing Rock

Cheyenne River

Ȟé Sápa

Say which oyáŋke and which town you are from.

Lower Brulé

Crow Creek

Pine Ridge

Yankton

Rosebud

Háu, Bob emáčiyapi.
Wazí Aháŋhaŋ él wathí.
Kyle él wathí.

Háŋ, Lisa emáčiyapi.
Sičháŋǧu Oyáŋke él wathí.
Mission él wathí.

8 Where did these itȟáŋčhaŋ settle?

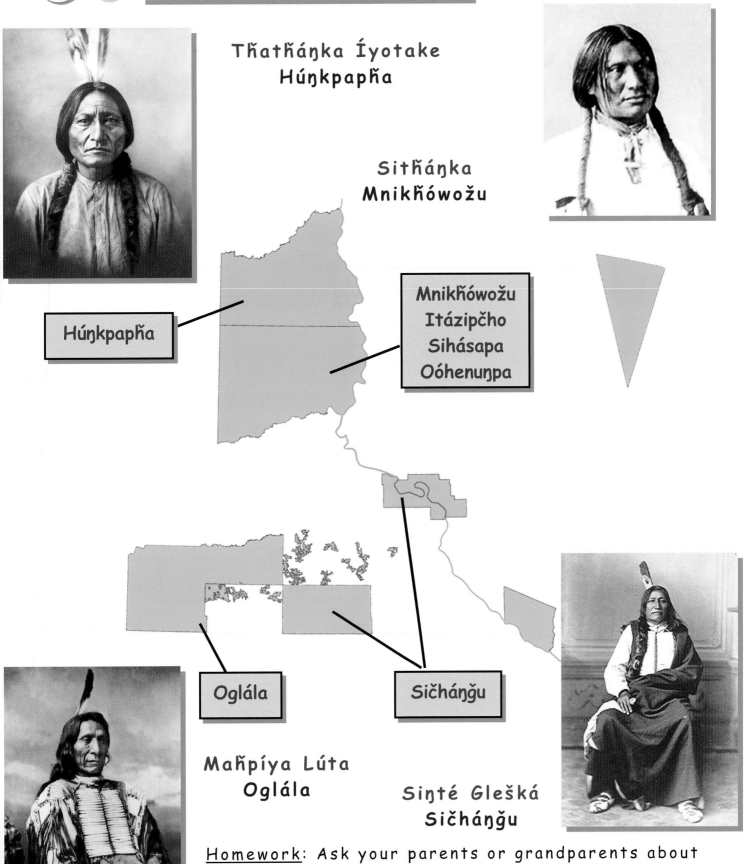

Tȟatȟáŋka Íyotake
Húŋkpapȟa

Sitȟáŋka
Mnikȟówožu

Húŋkpapȟa

Mnikȟówožu
Itázipčho
Sihásapa
Oóhenuŋpa

Oglála

Sičháŋǧu

Maȟpíya Lúta
Oglála

Siŋté Gleššká
Sičháŋǧu

Homework: Ask your parents or grandparents about
your ancestors and family tree.
Which of the seven Lakota tribes do you come from?
Do you have relatives from other tribes?

9 Oral or nasal vowels?

🔊 Listen and fill in a or aŋ

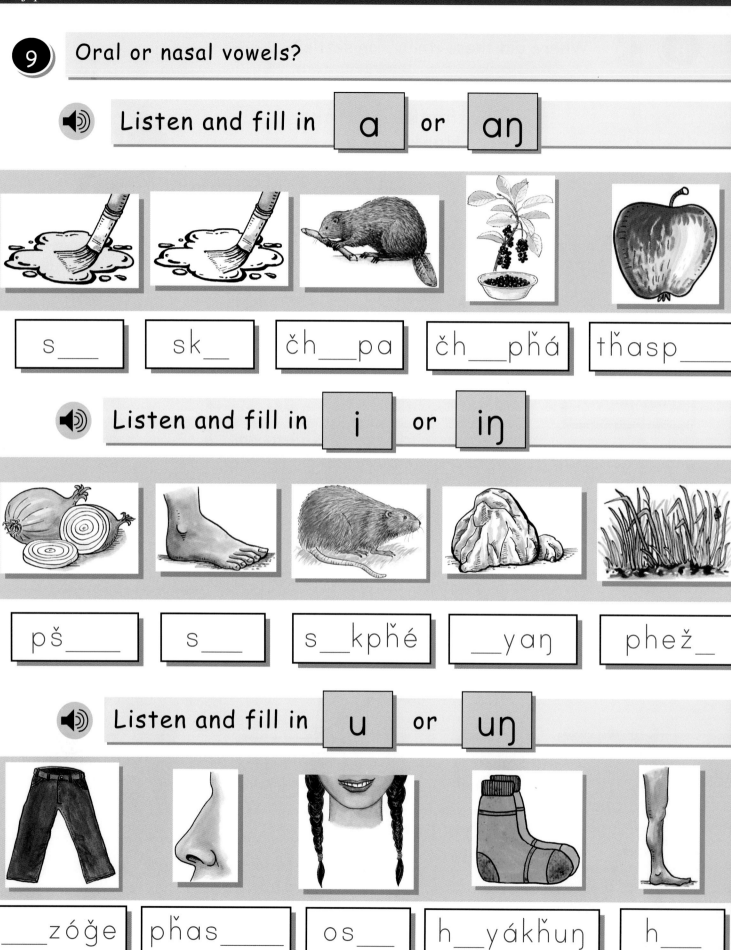

s___   sk_   čh__pa   čh__pȟá   tȟasp____

🔊 Listen and fill in i or iŋ

pš____   s___   s__kpȟé   __yaŋ   pȟež_

🔊 Listen and fill in u or uŋ

___zóǧe   pȟas____   os__   h_yákȟuŋ   h__

10 What are their names? Listen and fill in the names.

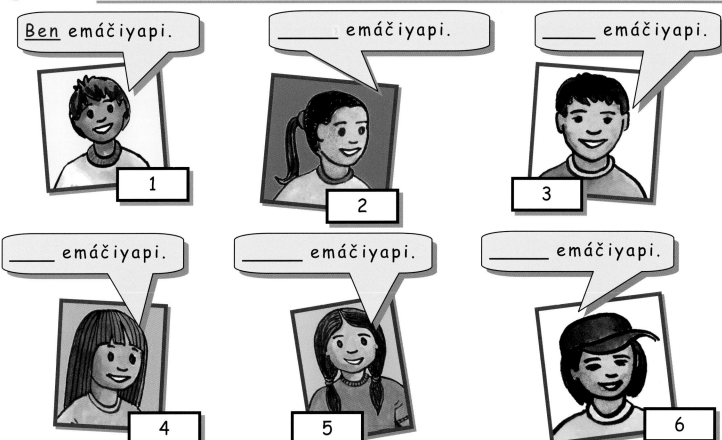

Ben emáčiyapi.

_____ emáčiyapi.

_____ emáčiyapi.

1

2

3

_____ emáčiyapi.

_____ emáčiyapi.

_____ emáčiyapi.

4

5

6

11 Can you finish the sentences about their names? Use the numbers next to the pictures to help you finish the sentences below.

1. Hokšíla kiŋ   **Ben**   ečíyapi.   The boy's name is Ben.

2. Wičhíŋčala kiŋ   ečíyapi.   The girl's name is   .

3. Hokšíla kiŋ   ečíyapi.   The boy's name is   .

4. Wičhíŋčala kiŋ   ečíyapi.   _____

5. Wičhíŋčala kiŋ   .   _____

6. Hokšíla kiŋ   .   _____

12 Learning about the stress mark.

Listen. What is the difference?

lená	léna
oglé	ógle
upí	úpi
waglí	wágli
yamní	yámni

á á á _____

é é é _____

í í í _____

ó ó ó _____

ú ú ú _____

áŋ áŋ áŋ _____

íŋ íŋ íŋ _____

úŋ úŋ úŋ _____

 13 Listen and fill in the stress mark on the first vowel:

píško	čhapa	šuŋka	tȟaȟča	kheya

 14 Listen and fill in the stress mark on the second vowel:

maká	hiŋhaŋ	igmu	gnaška	matȟo

Listen to each word and fill in the stress mark on the proper vowel.

heča   bloza   ziča   ȟoka   wabloša

4

topa   paha   wožapi   wata   ȟota

wazi   kimimela   išta   ičalu   ičabu

ogle   haŋpa   maǧa   sapa   šina

16 Read about Tina and then answer the questions below about yourself. Mark your hometown on the map.

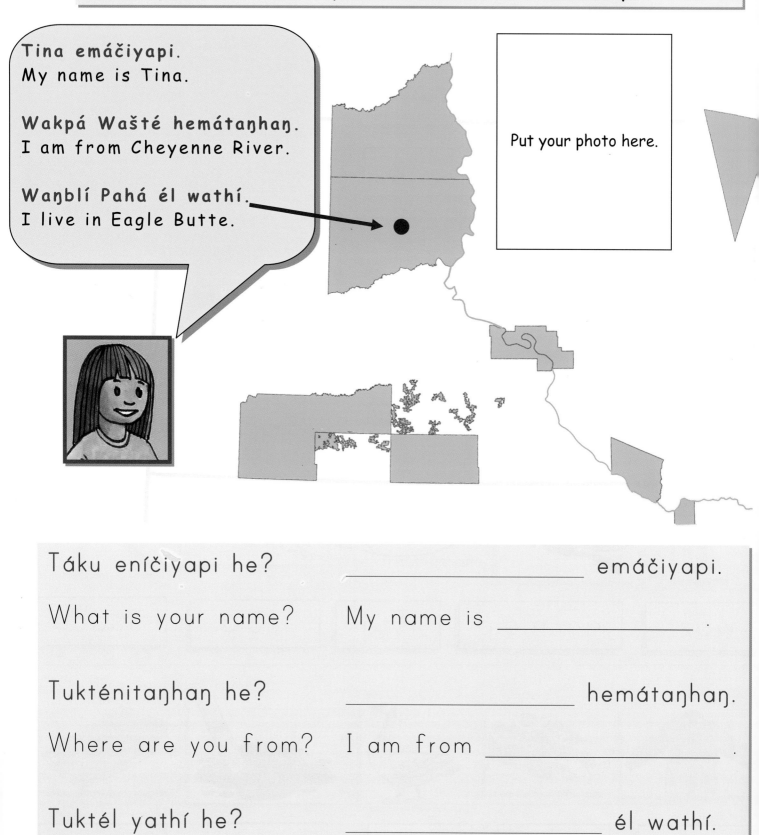

Tina emáčiyapi.
My name is Tina.

Wakpá Wašté hemátaŋhaŋ.
I am from Cheyenne River.

Waŋblí Pahá él wathí.
I live in Eagle Butte.

Put your photo here.

Táku eníčiyapi he? _____ emáčiyapi.

What is your name? My name is _____.

Tukténitaŋhaŋ he? _____ hemátaŋhaŋ.

Where are you from? I am from _____.

Tuktél yathí he? _____ él wathí.

Where do you live? I live in _____.

Reading and writing Lakota **č**.
The letter **č** makes a sound that is somewhere between the English **ch** in **rich** and the English **j** in **jar**. Listen and repeat.

Č č

čónala **(few)**

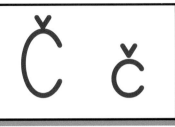

ča ča ča	čaŋ čaŋ
če če	
či či	čiŋ čiŋ
čo čo	
ču ču	čuŋ čuŋ

Reading and writing Lakota **čh**.
The letters **čh** make a sound that is like the English **ch** in **chair**. Listen and repeat.

ČH čh

čhápa

čha čha čha	čhaŋ čhaŋ
čhe čhe	
čhi čhi	čhiŋ čhiŋ
čho čho	
čhu čhu	čhuŋ čhuŋ

19 Listen and point to what you hear.

ča	če	či	čo	ču	čaŋ	čiŋ	čuŋ
čha	čhe	čhi	čho	čhu	čhaŋ	čhiŋ	čhuŋ

20 Listen and fill in č

    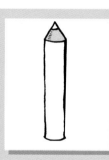

í_alu	zi_á	he_á	uŋ_í	wí_azo

21 Listen and fill in čh

__éǧa	__aŋté	__aŋwápe	__ápa	wi__áša

22 🔊 Listen and fill in **č** or **čh**

   **10**

| __aŋpȟá | __aŋkú | __áŋ | wik__émna | i__ábu |

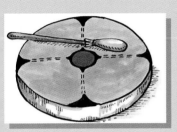   

| __áŋčheǧa | uŋk__éla | tȟáȟ__a | __uwígnaka |

| waȟ__á | wahá__aŋka | omní__a | wakší__a |

| __éya | uŋk__ékiȟa | __egnáke | thiík__eya |

2 Lé táku hwo/he? What is this?

Lé tȟatȟáŋka héčha.

Lé šúŋka héčha.

pispíza

khéya

šuŋgmánitu

maká

niǧésaŋla

šúŋkawakȟaŋ

igmú

itȟúŋkala

maštíŋska

matȟó

iktómi

heȟáka

gnaška kimímela

čhápa

2 🔊 Repeat the dialog using each of the animals.

3 🔊 The letter s in Lakota sounds like the English **s** in <u>sit</u>.

Ss

sí

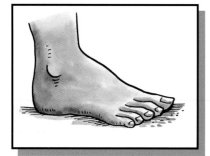

sa sa sa   saŋ saŋ saŋ

se se

si si   siŋ siŋ

so so

su su   suŋ suŋ

4 🔊 The letter š in Lakota sounds like the English **sh** in <u>share</u>.

Šš

šúŋka

ša ša ša   šaŋ šaŋ šaŋ

še še

ši ši   šiŋ šiŋ

šo šo

šu šu   šuŋ šuŋ

5   Listen and fill in S or Š

| _ká | _á | a_áŋpi | wáblo_a | wáblo_ka |

| p_íŋ | p_íŋ | i_tá | i_tó | hok_íla |

7

| _akówiŋ | _iŋtéȟla | tȟa_páŋ | khukhú_e | _iŋkpȟé |

| gna_ká | pí_ko | oí_e yámni | wak_íča | čhúŋ_oke |

6 Háŋ and hiyá (Yes and no).

Lé **šúŋka** héčha hwo?

Háŋ.

Lé **šúŋka** héčha he?

Hiyá.

Listen to and read the dialog. Can you guess what they are saying?
Try to answer the following questions.

What do boys say at the end of a question? _____

What do girls say at the end of a question? _____

How do we say "YES" in Lakota? _____

How do we say "NO" in Lakota? _____

7 Repeat the dialog with your classmates using the pictures and
words below.

| igmú ? | kimímela ? | waŋblí ? | šúŋkawakȟáŋ ? | šúŋka ? |

8 Answer the questions by circling **háŋ** or **hiyá**.

Lé **šúŋka** héčha hwo/he? (háŋ) hiyá

Lé **igmú** héčha hwo/he? háŋ (hiyá)

Lé **matȟó** héčha hwo/he? háŋ hiyá

Lé **kimímela** héčha hwo/he? háŋ hiyá

Lé **šuŋgmánitu** héčha hwo/he? háŋ hiyá

Lé **tȟatȟáŋka** héčha hwo/he? háŋ hiyá

Lé **maká** héčha hwo/he? háŋ hiyá

Lé **pispíza** héčha hwo/he? háŋ hiyá

Lé **siŋtéȟla** héčha hwo/he? háŋ hiyá

Lé **gnaška** héčha hwo/he? háŋ hiyá

9 The letter **z** in Lakota sounds like the English **z** in **z**ero.

Z z

zičá

za za za	zaŋ zaŋ
ze ze	
zi zi	ziŋ ziŋ
zo zo	
zu zu	zuŋ zuŋ

10 The letter **ž** in Lakota sounds like the English **z** in a**z**ure.

Ž ž

žó

ža ža ža	žaŋ žaŋ
že že	
ži ži	žiŋ žiŋ
žo žo	
žu žu	žuŋ žuŋ

11 🔊 Listen and fill in **z** or **ž**

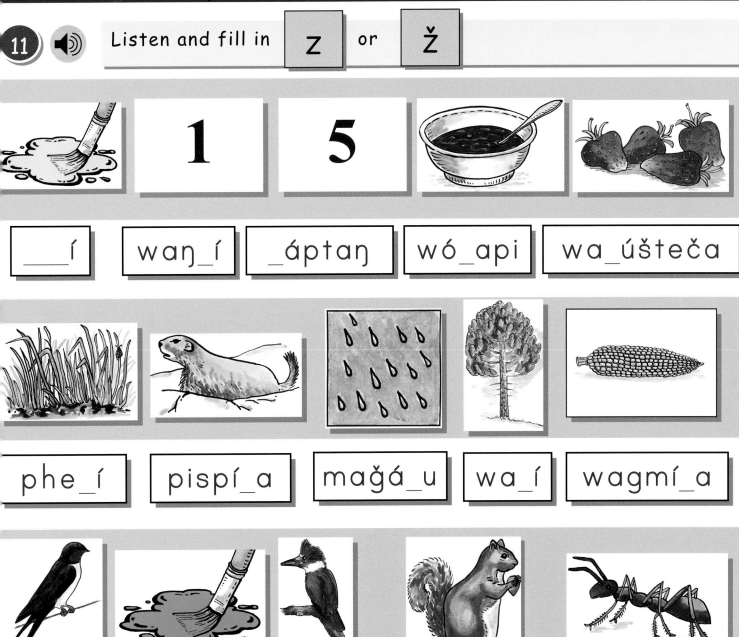

__í	waŋ_í	_áptaŋ	wó_api	wa_úšteča

phe_í	pispí_a	maǧá_u	wa_í	wagmí_a

upí_ata	tȟó_i	hoyá_ela	_ičá	tȟa_úška

_íškopela	wó_uha	uŋ_óǧe	o_áŋ_aŋglepi

12 Making a negative sentence.

Lé **šúŋka** héčha hwo?

Hiyá, lé **šúŋka** héčha <u>šni</u>.

šúŋka ?

Lé **igmú** héčha.

Listen to the dialog. Can you guess what Bob and Lisa are saying? How does Lisa say "**NOT**"? Where is this in a sentence?

13 Read Bob and Lisa's examples. Make similar "NOT" sentences using the pictures and the crossed out words.

Lé **igmú** héčha šni.

Lé **gnaška** héčha šni.

~~matȟó~~

~~čhápa~~

khéya

igmú

gnaška

~~pispíza~~

šúŋka

~~kimímela~~

maká

~~tȟatȟáŋka~~

14 Circle the correct sentence as in the examples.

Lé **tȟatȟáŋka** héčha. Lé **tȟatȟáŋka** héčha šni.

Lé **tȟáȟča** héčha. Lé **tȟáȟča** héčha šni.

Lé **šúŋka** héčha. Lé **šúŋka** héčha šni.

Lé **pispíza** héčha. Lé **pispíza** héčha šni.

Lé **niǧésaŋla** héčha. Lé **niǧésaŋla** héčha šni.

Lé **waŋblí** héčha. Lé **waŋblí** héčha šni.

Lé **heȟáka** héčha. Lé **heȟáka** héčha šni.

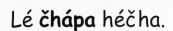

Lé **čhápa** héčha. Lé **čhápa** héčha šni.

Lé **maká** héčha. Lé **maká** héčha šni.

Lé **khéya** héčha. Lé **khéya** héčha šni.

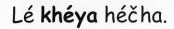

15 There are 22 animals in the word-find. Can you find them?

š	úŋ	k	a	p	kh	é	y	a	p	s
uŋ	i	m	a	š	t	íŋ	s	k	a	iŋ
g	áŋ	tȟ	a	tȟ	áŋ	k	a	i	ž	t
m	m	š	úŋ	k	a	w	a	kȟ	áŋ	é
á	iŋ	kh	i	k	t	ó	m	i	p	ȟ
n	tȟ	á	ȟ	č	a	ǧ	a	p	é	l
i	g	m	ú	t	a	l	m	i	l	a
t	w	a	š	t	e	l	a	s	m	g
u	aŋ	tȟ	a	m	a	čh	á	p	a	n
ȟ	b	ó	í	pȟ	a	h	íŋ	í	k	a
a	l	m	kȟ	aŋ	ǧ	í	m	z	á	š
p	i	h	e	ȟ	á	k	a	a	š	k
k	n	i	ǧ	é	s	aŋ	l	a	t	á

16 Decide which animals are **tȟáŋka** - big and which are **čík'ala** - small.

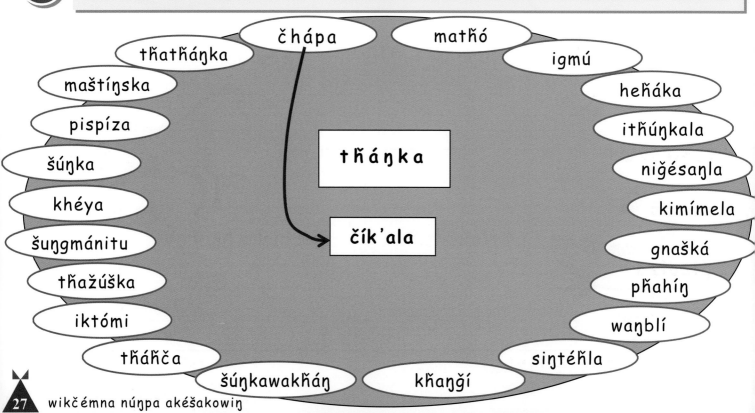

čhápa — matȟó — tȟatȟáŋka — igmú — maštíŋska — heȟáka — pispíza — itȟúŋkala — šúŋka — niǧésaŋla — khéya — kimímela — šuŋgmánitu — gnaška — tȟažúška — pȟahíŋ — iktómi — waŋblí — tȟáȟča — siŋtéȟla — šúŋkawakȟáŋ — kȟaŋǧí

tȟáŋka

čík'ala

17 Connect the animals that begin with the same letter.

18 Which animals eat grass - **pheží** and which eat meat - **tȟáló?**

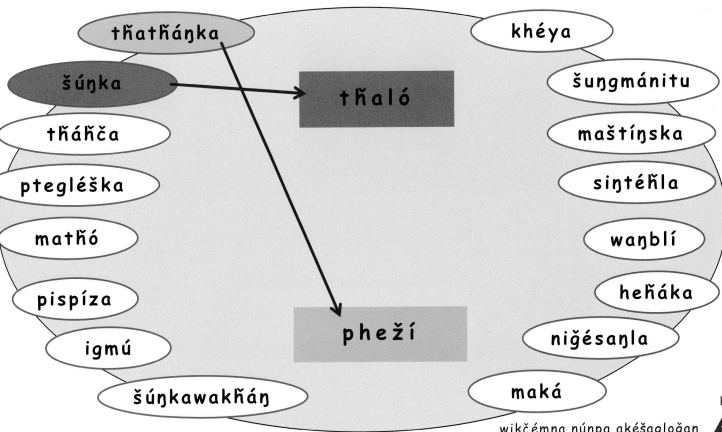

tȟatȟáŋka

khéya

šúŋka

šuŋgmánitu

tȟáló

tȟáȟča

maštíŋska

ptegléška

siŋtéȟla

matȟó

waŋblí

pispíza

heȟáka

pheží

igmú

niǧésaŋla

šúŋkawakȟáŋ

maká

3   Lé naíŋš hé?   This or that?

1 🔊 Listen and point at the words you hear. Put each word in a sentence just like Bob.

wówapi   thiyópa   wóžuha   akáŋwowapi   wakšíča

oákaŋke

wíyukse

itówapi

wíčazo   wíyatke   čhaŋbláska   wíyaskabye

Lé thiyópa héčha.

šúŋka

matȟó

2 Connect the two halves and match them with the words.

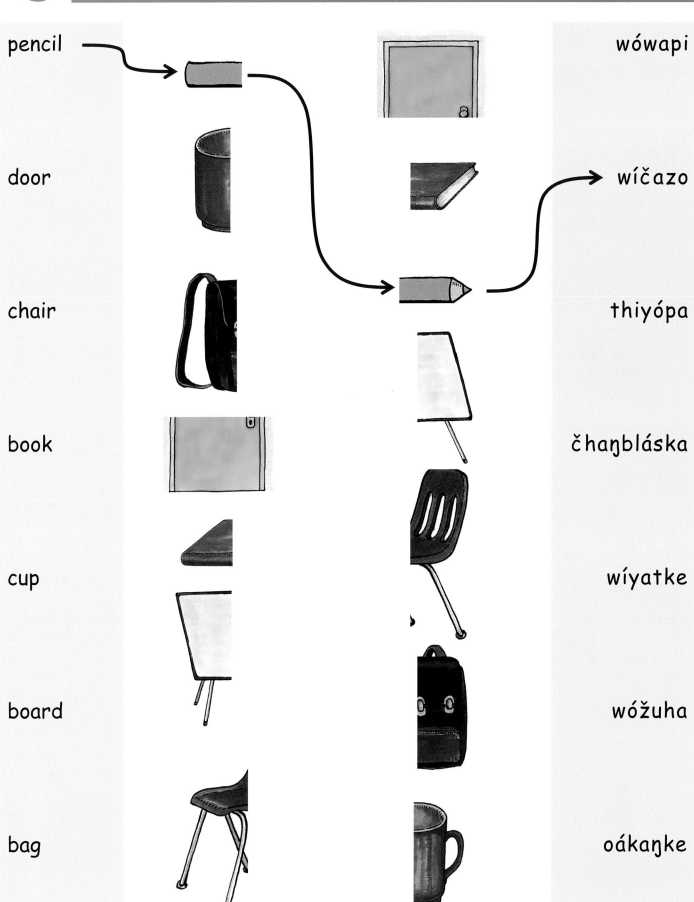

pencil

door

chair

book

cup

board

bag

wówapi

wíčazo

thiyópa

čhaŋbláska

wíyatke

wóžuha

oákaŋke

3 🔊 | Reading and writing **k, p, t** (plain stops).

The letter **k** sounds like the English **k** in s<u>k</u>ill.
Listen and repeat: ská, šúŋka, kíza, maká, okó, škáta, kimímela

K k

ka ka ka	kaŋ kaŋ kaŋ
ke ke	
ki ki	kiŋ kiŋ
ko ko	
ku ku	kuŋ kuŋ

kimímela

The letter **p** sounds like the English **p** in s<u>p</u>ill or in ha<u>pp</u>y.
Listen and repeat: sápa, spáya, púza, pispíza, núŋpa, tópa

P p

pa pa pa	paŋ paŋ paŋ
pe pe	
pi pi	piŋ piŋ
po po	
pu pu	puŋ puŋ

pispíza

The letter **t** sounds like the English **t** in **st̲ill**.
Listen and repeat: táku, tóna, stáka, tuwé, tópa

T t

tópa

4

ta ta ta ___   taŋ taŋ taŋ ___

te te ___

ti ti ___   tiŋ tiŋ ___

to to ___

tu tu ___   tuŋ tuŋ ___

4   🔊   Listen and fill in   **k**   **p**   and   **t**

k

_imímela   čhaŋš_á   gnaš_á   ma_á

p

_ispíza   _íško   u_ížata   čhá_a

t

4

__ópa   maš_íŋska   ma_úška   ik_ómi

5 The teacher, Mrs. Spotted Elk, needs to know how many school supplies she has in her classroom. Can you help her? How many objects can you find? Write the numbers next to the words below.

oákaŋke __3__	wíyatke ____	akáŋwowapi ____	wóžuha ____
wówapi ____	wíyukse ____	wíyaskabye ____	wíčazo ____
itówapi ____	thiyópa ____	wakšíča ____	waȟčá ____

6 🔊 Listen and fill in the proper letter **k** **p** or **t**

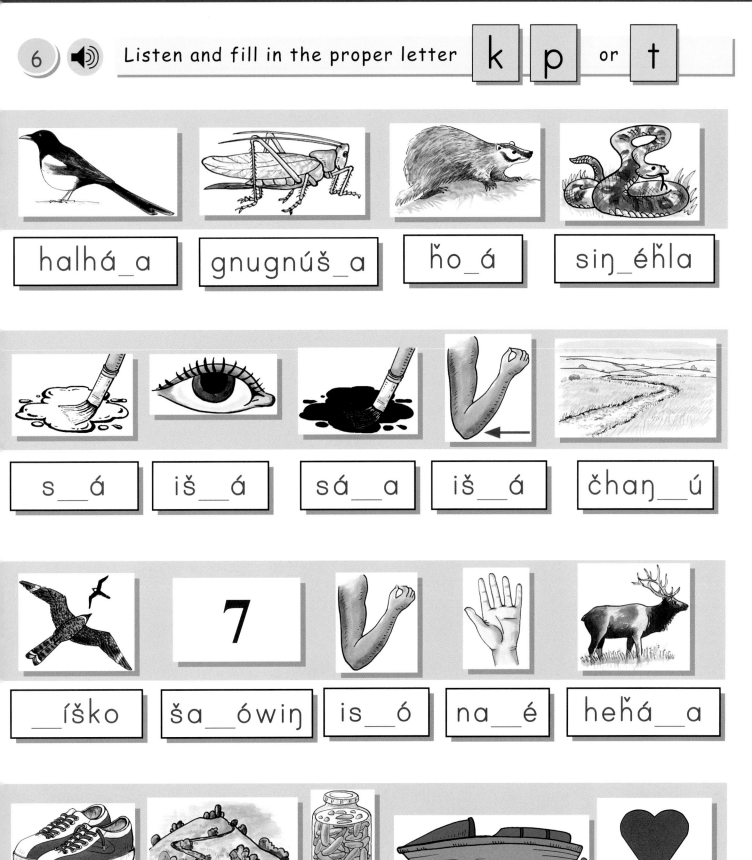

halhá_a   gnugnúš_a   ȟo_á   siŋ_éȟla

s__á   iš__á   sá__a   iš__á   čhaŋ__ú

__íško   ša__ówiŋ   is__ó   na__é   heȟá__a

hán__a   __ahá   _uŋ_úŋ   wá__a   čhaŋ_é

7 🔊 When do we say **lé** and when **hé**? This and that?

Lé **wóžuha** héčha.

Lé **thiyópa** héčha.

Hé **wóžuha** héčha.

Hé **thiyópa** héčha.

Lé **naíŋš** hé? (This or that?). What is the rule?

When something is near and we can touch it we say _____ .
When something is far and we cannot touch it we say _____ .

Lé **wíyatke** héčha.

Hé **wíyatke** héčha.

8 Fill in **lé** or **hé**. This or that. Use the hand to help you.

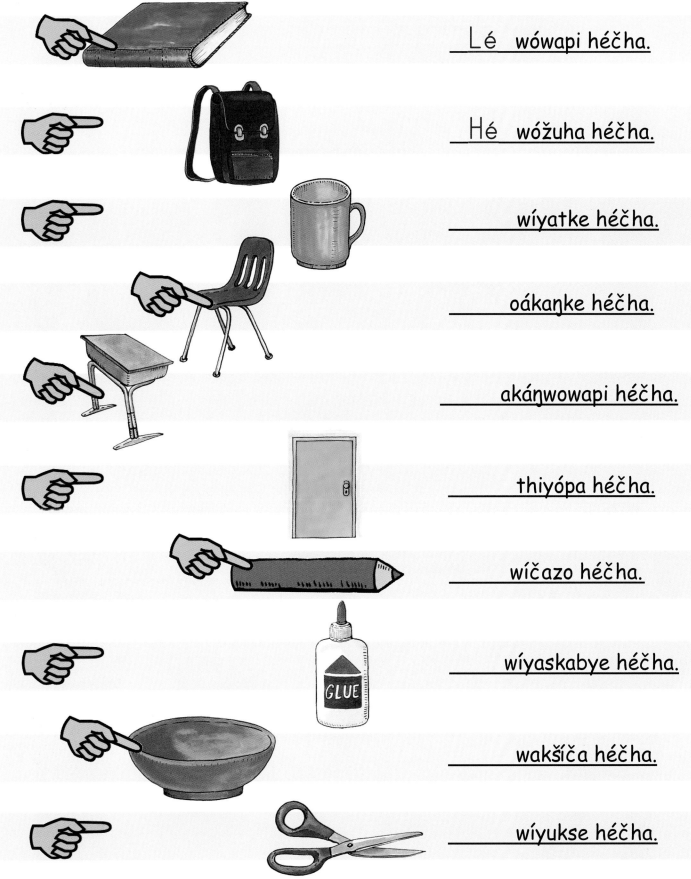

_Lé_ wówapi héčha.

_Hé_ wóžuha héčha.

_____ wíyatke héčha.

_____ oákaŋke héčha.

_____ akáŋwowapi héčha.

_____ thiyópa héčha.

_____ wíčazo héčha.

_____ wíyaskabye héčha.

_____ wakšíča héčha.

_____ wíyukse héčha.

9 Find a partner and repeat Bob and Lisa's dialog touching other classroom objects. Make sure you use **lé** when you ask and touch and **hé** when you reply.

Lé táku hwo?

Hé oákaŋke héčha.

10 Find a partner and repeat Lisa and Bob's dialog using animal flashcards. Use **lé** in the question and **hé** in the answer.

Lé táku he?

Hé niǧésaŋla héčha.

11) Find a partner and repeat Lisa and Bob's guessing game using animal flashcards hidden behind your back. Use **lé** in the question and **hé** in the answer.

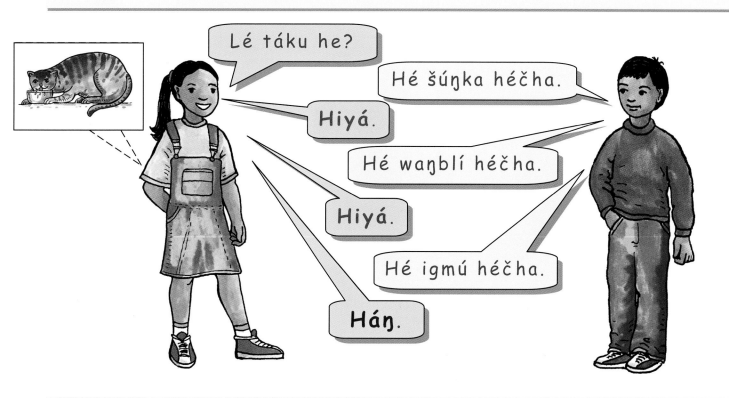

12) What are they asking Bob and Lisa to do?

13 Crossword.

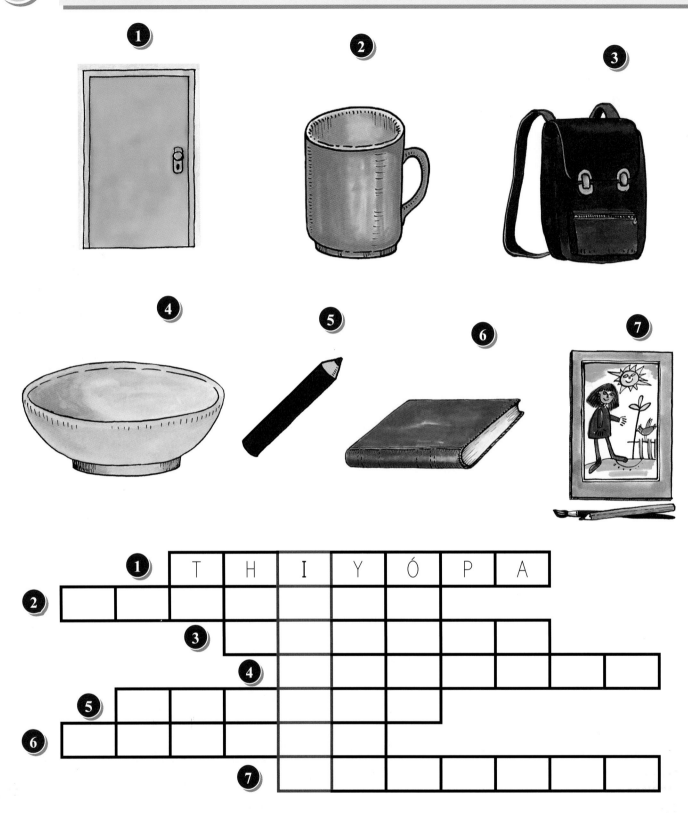

Finish the crossword to find out what Lisa brought to the classroom today.

14 There are 14 hidden words. Can you find them?

a	y	ú	w	i	čh	íŋ	č	a	l	a	g	b
w	a	k	w	i	t	ó	w	a	p	i	a	t
a	w	w	ó	w	a	p	i	í	b	k	ȟ	h
n	a	u	ž	l	a	t	h	aŋ	č	iŋ	é	n
o	k	th	u	w	a	t	ú	k	l	a	h	o
p	š	i	h	o	k	š	í	l	a	uŋ	z	u
w	í	y	a	s	k	a	b	y	e	g	k	o
a	č	ó	n	m	i	p	o	á	k	aŋ	k	e
ȟ	a	p	a	w	í	y	u	k	s	e	n	z
č	e	a	w	í	y	a	t	k	e	g	é	y
á	t	aŋ	l	é	g	s	u	p	a	k	e	l

15 Draw a circle around the animals and a rectangle around the things.

wówapi	pispíza	akáŋwowapi	igmú

khéya   šúŋkawakȟáŋ   kimímela   wíčazo

itówapi   wíyukse   ťȟatȟáŋka

wakšíča

maká   oákaŋke   heȟáka

šuŋgmánitu

wíyaskabye   thiyópa

wóžuha

ťȟáȟča   wíyatke   gnašká

čhápa

4 Waníyetu nitóna hwo/he? How old are you?

1 Listen, repeat and fill in the missing numbers.

1	2	3	4		
waŋží	núŋpa	yámni	tópa	záptaŋ	šákpe

šakówiŋ	šaglóǧaŋ	napčíyuŋka	wikčémna	akéwaŋži	akénuŋpa

Match the numbers.

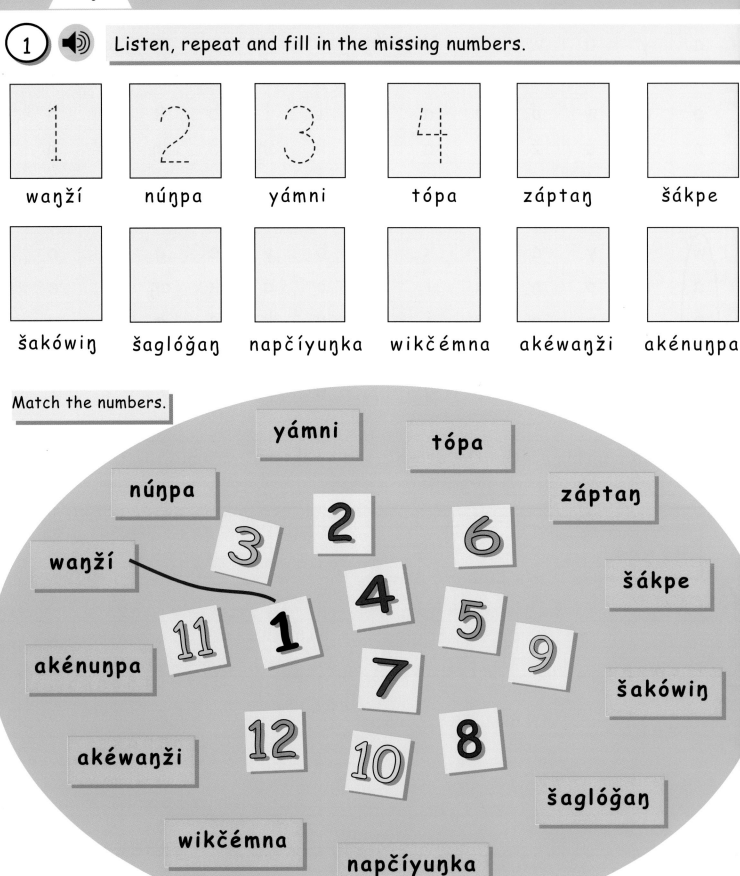

② Match each number with a picture and the proper phrase.

7

5

8

10

1

3

6

4

9

2

11

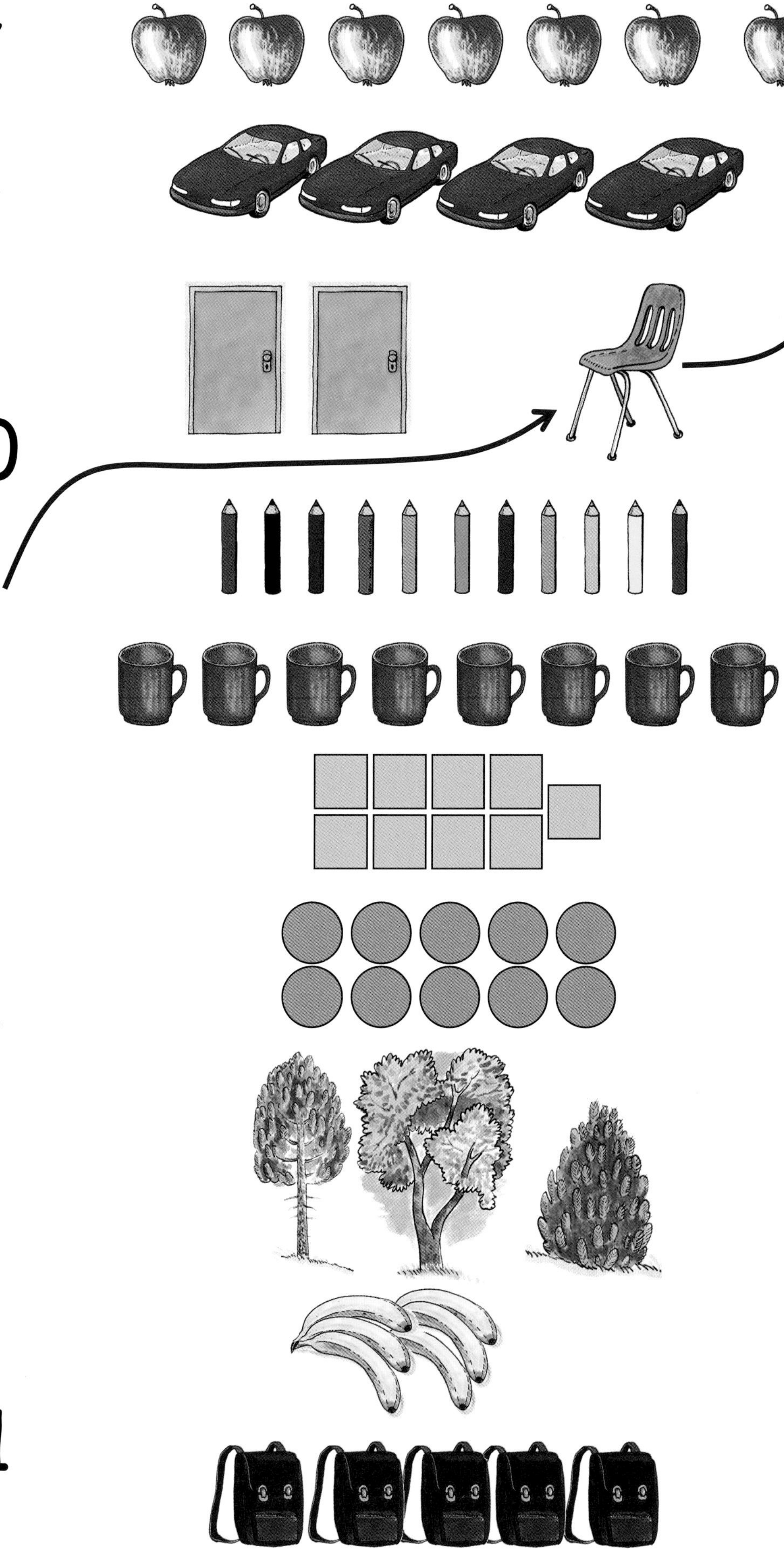

oákaŋke **waŋží**

thiyópa **núŋpa**

čháŋ **yámni**

iyéčhiŋkiŋyaŋke **tópa**

wóžuha **záptaŋ**

zíškopa **šákpe**

tȟaspáŋ **šakówiŋ**

wíyatke **šaglóǧaŋ**

oblótȟuŋ **napčíyuŋka**

mimémla **wikčémna**

wíčazo **akéwaŋži**

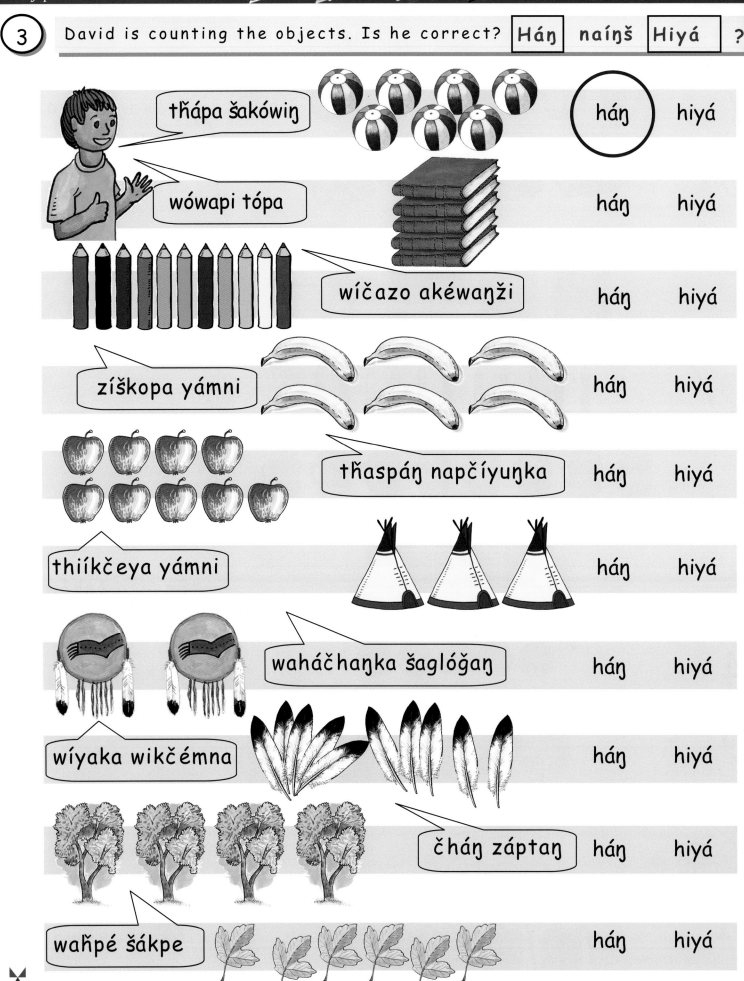

4 Can you find all the words for numbers?

m	w	a	n	í	y	e	t	u
u	w	i	k	č	é	m	n	a
n	z	a	š	a	k	ó	w	iŋ
úŋ	á	t	aŋ	w	a	t	e	l
p	p	š	a	g	l	ó	ǧ	aŋ
a	t	i	š	á	k	p	e	k
w	aŋ	ž	í	m	k	a	g	l
n	a	p	č	í	y	uŋ	k	a
a	m	y	á	m	n	i	č	e
š	a	k	é	w	aŋ	ž	i	l

waŋží
n̶ú̶ŋ̶p̶a̶
yámni
tópa
záptaŋ
šákpe
šakówiŋ
šaglóǧaŋ
napčíyuŋka
wikčémna
akéwaŋži

5 Listen. What is the teacher asking Bob and Lisa to do?

Iyáya ye!

Wówapi kiŋ yuǧáŋ ye!

6 🔊 Reading and writing **h**.

H h

hokšíla

ḣa ḣa ḣa	haŋ haŋ haŋ
ḣe ḣe	
ḣi ḣi	hiŋ hiŋ
ḣo ḣo	
ḣu ḣu	huŋ huŋ

7 🔊 Reading and writing **ȟ**.

Ȟ ȟ

ȟé

ȟa ȟa ȟa	ȟaŋ ȟaŋ ȟaŋ
ȟe ȟe	
ȟi ȟi	ȟiŋ ȟiŋ
ȟo ȟo	
ȟu ȟu	ȟuŋ ȟuŋ

(8) Listen and fill in **h** or **ȟ**

_okšíla	_é	_oká	_oká	_ú

_áŋpa	wa_čá	_oyázela	_ečá	_óta

ma_píya	_uŋská	wičhá_pi	_í	_iŋháŋ

wa_pé	_alháta	siŋté_la	ma_éluŋpi

9 How old are they? Read and listen to the children below.

Waníyetu <u>nitóna</u> hwo?

Tina

Waníyetu <u>mašákowiŋ</u>.

Waníyetu <u>nitóna</u> he?

David

Waníyetu <u>mašákpe</u>.

How old is Tina? _____ (write the number)
How old is David? _____ (write the number)

How old are you?
Waníyetu ma_____.
(write the number in Lakota)

Connect the parts of the sentence that match:

<u>Waníyetu</u>   <u>nitóna</u>   <u>he</u>?

<u>how many you are</u> / <u>question</u> / <u>winters (years)</u>

Ask your classmates their age in Lakota.

10 How old are they? Read what they say and complete the sentences below.

Tina waníyetu šakówiŋ.   Tina is seven years old.

Tom waníyetu

Mary waníyetu

Ben waníyetu

Lucy waníyetu

Miyé waníyetu ma   I am   years old.

11 What time is it?

When we ask the time in Lakota, we can use either **mázaškaŋškaŋ** or **owápȟe** (and also **oápȟe**) for 'hour'. Find a partner and repeat the dialog pointing to all the clocks on the next page.

12 Write the numbers in Lakota.

1 waŋží

5

8

2

9

11

7

4

3

6

12

10

(13) What is your phone number?

Tina, omás'apȟe nitȟáwa tókča he?

šaglóǧaŋ – šákpe – šakówiŋ
núŋpa – záptaŋ – tákuni - šaglóǧaŋ

Tina: šaglóǧaŋ-šákpe-šakówiŋ – núŋpa-záptaŋ-tákuni-šaglóǧaŋ

Tina's phone number is: 8 6 7 – 2 5 0 8

Tom: šaglóǧaŋ-záptaŋ-šákpe - núŋpa-waŋží-šákpe-tákuni

Tom's number is: _____

Mary: napčíyuŋka-šákpe-tópa – núŋpa-šakówiŋ-tákuni-yámni

Mary's number is: _____

Ben: záptaŋ-yámni-šaglóǧaŋ – tópa-šakówiŋ-napčíyuŋka-záptaŋ

Ben's number is: _____

Lucy: šaglóǧaŋ-núŋpa-yámni – waŋží-šákpe-tákuni-šakówiŋ

Lucy's number is: _____

My friend:

My friend's number is: _____

Me:

My number is:_____

14 Connect the numbers from 1 to 15 to discover Bob's favorite animal.

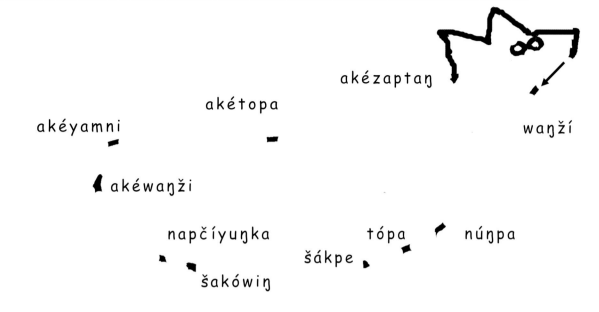

akézaptaŋ

akétopa

akéyamni

waŋží

akéwaŋži

napčíyuŋka

tópa

núŋpa

šákpe

šakówiŋ

akénuŋpa

yámni

wikčémna

šaglóǧaŋ

záptaŋ

15 Can you add and subtract in Lakota? Fill in the answers below.

waŋží	+	tópa	=	záptaŋ
akénuŋpa	-	wikčémna	=	
šakówiŋ	+	záptaŋ	=	
wikčémna	-	šakówiŋ	=	
núŋpa	+	napčíyuŋka	=	
šaglóǧaŋ	-	šákpe	=	
yámni	+	tópa	=	
akéwaŋži	-	šakówiŋ	=	

16 Three of the four words are related. Which word does not belong on each line?

tópa	waŋží	heȟáka	wikčémna
wówapi	igmú	wóžuha	oákaŋke
pispíza	čhápa	kimímela	šakówiŋ
šúŋka	napčíyuŋka	šaglóǧaŋ	yámni

5 Tȟaspáŋ waštéwalake. I like apples.

1 🔊 Lisa and Bob went grocery shopping. Listen and match the pictures with the words.

Lisa:

- tȟaspáŋ tópa
- bló záptaŋ
- pšíŋ šákpe
- wažúšteča akénuŋpa
- tȟaspáŋzi napčíyuŋka
- thíŋpsiŋla waŋží

Bob:

- pȟaŋǧí zizí yámni
- kȟáŋta šaglóǧaŋ
- wagmúšpaŋšni núŋpa
- zíškopela šakówiŋ
- uŋžíŋžiŋtka akéwaŋži
- wagmíza wikčémna

2 Can you match the pictures with the words?

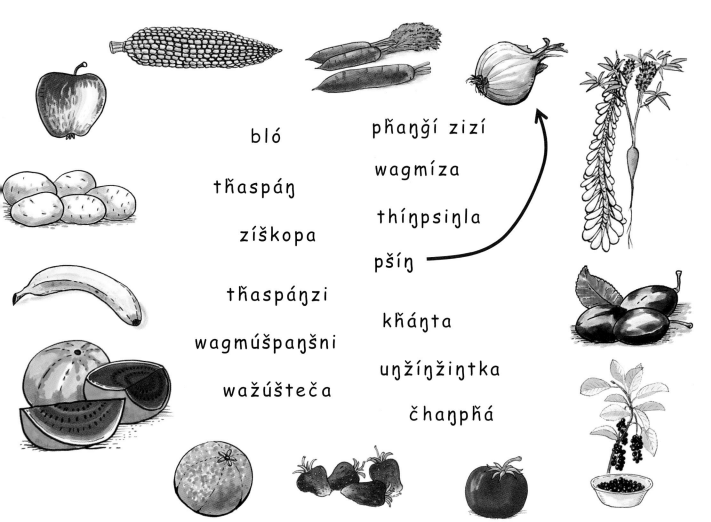

bló

tȟaspáŋ

zíškopa

tȟaspáŋzi

wagmúšpaŋšni

wažúšteča

pȟaŋǧí zizí

wagmíza

tȟíŋpsiŋla

pšíŋ

kȟáŋta

uŋžíŋžiŋtka

čhaŋpȟá

3 Mary likes plums. Draw a picture of a food you like and write its name.

Kȟáŋta waštéwalake.

Mary

_____ waštéwalake.

I like_____.

4)) Read and listen to the children. What do they like?

Táku waštéyalaka hwo?

Tina

Tȟaspáŋ waštéwalake.

Tina tȟaspáŋ waštélake. – Tina likes apples.

Táku waštéyalaka he?

Brian

Asáŋpi waštéwalake.

Brian asáŋpi waštélake. – Brian likes milk.

Look at the children above. They are asking each other about what they like.

How do you say "YOU LIKE" in Lakota?   wašté___lake

How do you say "I LIKE" in Lakota?   wašté___lake

How do you say "HE/SHE LIKES" in Lakota?   _____

5 What do you like? Find a partner and repeat the children's dialog used in the examples.

6 Who likes what? Match the person with the food. Then try to complete the sentences below.

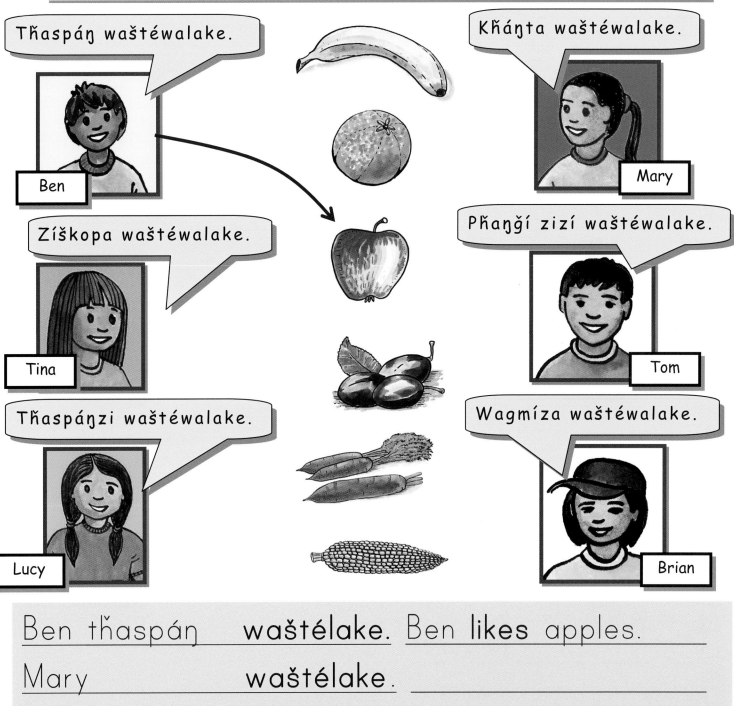

Tȟaspáŋ waštéwalake.

Ben

Zíškopa waštéwalake.

Tina

Tȟaspáŋzi waštéwalake.

Lucy

Kȟáŋta waštéwalake.

Mary

Pȟaŋǧí zizí waštéwalake.

Tom

Wagmíza waštéwalake.

Brian

Ben tȟaspáŋ   waštélake.   Ben **likes** apples.

Mary   waštélake.   _____

Tina   waštélake.   _____

Tom   .   _____

Lucy   .   _____

Brian   .   _____

7 🔊 Reading and writing kȟ, pȟ, tȟ.

Reading and writing kȟ.

kȟ

kȟáŋta

kȟa kȟa kȟa kȟa
kȟe kȟe
kȟo kȟo
kȟaŋ kȟaŋ
kȟuŋ kȟuŋ

Reading and writing pȟ.

pȟ

pȟahíŋ

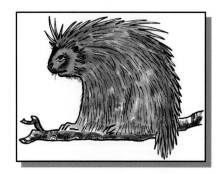

pȟa pȟa pȟa
pȟe pȟe
pȟo pȟo
pȟaŋ pȟaŋ
pȟuŋ pȟuŋ

Reading and writing **tȟ**.

tȟ

__tȟ__atȟáŋka

tȟa   tȟa   tȟa

tȟe   tȟe

tȟo   tȟo

tȟaŋ   tȟaŋ

tȟuŋ   tȟuŋ

(8) 🔊 Listen and fill in   **kȟ**   **pȟ**   and   **tȟ**

 kȟ

___áŋta   __okȟóyaȟ'aŋla   ___aŋǧí   ma__óčhe

 pȟ

 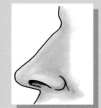  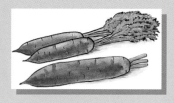

___ahíŋ   ___asú   čhaŋ__á   ___aŋǧí zizí

tȟ

__atȟáŋka   __ápa   ___ózi   ma__ó

9 The school cook, Mrs. Jumping Weasel, needs help counting her produce for lunch. Help her count the number of fruits and vegetables on the table and write the answers below.

zíškopela _záptaŋ_   wagmíza _____

tȟaspáŋzi _____   wagmúšpaŋšni _____

bló _____   tȟaspáŋ _____

kȟáŋta _____   wažúšteča _____

10 **Listen and and fill in** 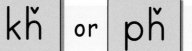 kȟ **or** pȟ **or** tȟ

La__óta   wa__óštaŋ   __ápa   čha___úŋka   __ó

__áŋta   __uŋkášila   __aŋǧí   __ašnáheča

__aspáŋ   __atkáša   __áȟča   siŋk__é   huŋyá__uŋ

__aló   __ahíŋ   __ašíyagnuŋpa   ma__á   __éta

11 Who likes milk? Some of Lisa's friends like milk and others do not. Read the dialog and then circle the correct answer in the sentences below.
Ask your classmates the same question.

Asáŋpi waštéyalaka he?

Ben — Háŋ.
Mary — Hiyá.
Tina — Hiyá.
Tom — Háŋ.
Lucy — Háŋ.
Brian — Hiyá.

(Ben asáŋpi waštélake.)	Ben asáŋpi waštélake šni.
(Ben likes milk.)	*(Ben doesn't like milk.)*
Mary asáŋpi waštélake.	**(Mary asáŋpi waštélake šni.)**
Tina asáŋpi waštélake.	Tina asáŋpi waštélake šni.
Tom asáŋpi waštélake.	Tom asáŋpi waštélake šni.
Lucy asáŋpi waštélake.	Lucy asáŋpi waštélake šni.
Brian asáŋpi waštélake.	Brian asáŋpi waštélake šni.

12 Match the pictures that begin with the same letter.

6 Oówa tókča hwo/he? — What color is it?

1 Listen, point at and repeat the words for colors.

ská · sáŋ · ȟóta · sápa · šá · tȟó · zí · ǧí

2 Mixing colors. Listen, read and repeat their names.

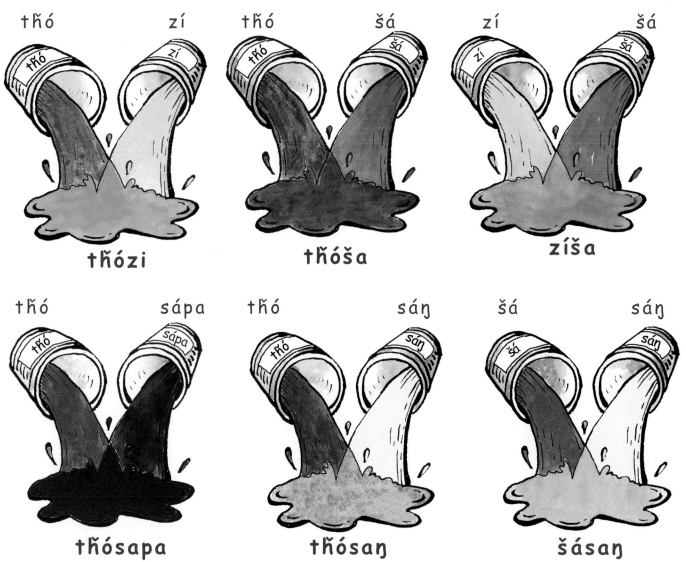

| tȟó + zí = tȟózi | tȟó + šá = tȟóša | zí + šá = zíša |
| tȟó + sápa = tȟósapa | tȟó + sáŋ = tȟósaŋ | šá + sáŋ = šásaŋ |

3 Fill in the colors to discover the dream Bob had last night.

4 "This is a black dog." "This is a blue book". Finish the sentences below.

Lé šúŋka **sápe**.

Lé wówapi **tȟó**.

Lé oákaŋke _____.

Lé _____ ǧí.

Lé _____ tȟózi.

Lé wówapi _____.

Lé wíyukse _____.

Lé _____ tȟó.

____ igmú ská.

Lé wíčazo _____.

Lé šúŋkawakȟaŋ _____.

Lé _____ šá.

___ _____ _____.

___ _____ _____.

5 🔊 Anáǧoptaŋ na eyá po! (Listen and repeat!)

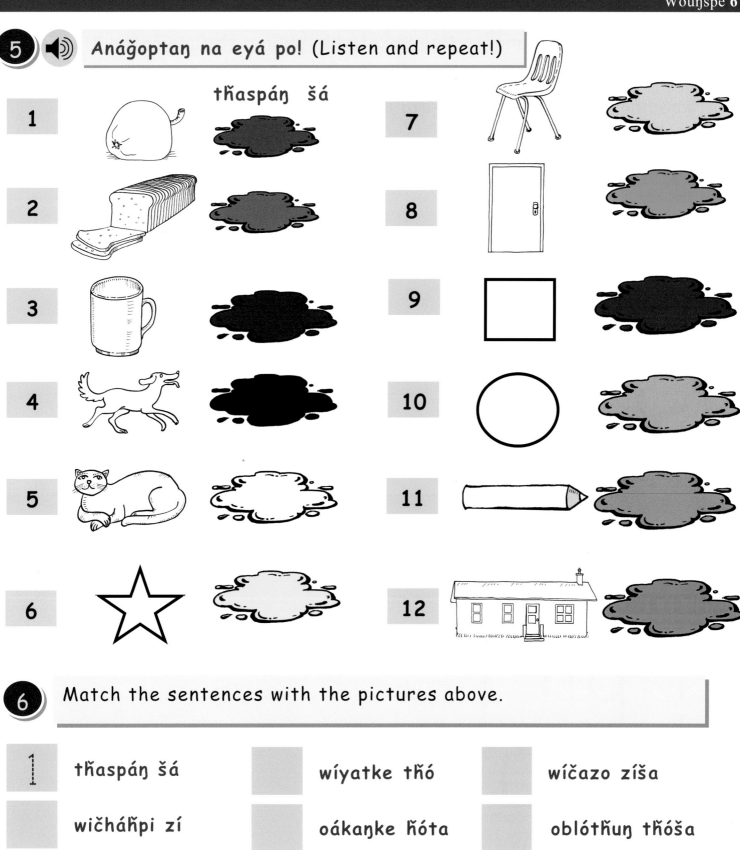

tȟaspáŋ šá

1

2

3

4

5

6

7

8

9

10

11

12

6 Match the sentences with the pictures above.

| 1 | tȟaspáŋ šá | | wíyatke tȟó | | wíčazo zíša |

| | wičháȟpi zí | | oákaŋke ȟóta | | oblótȟuŋ tȟóša |

| | igmú ská | | aǧúyapi ǧí | | šúŋka sápe |

| | Thípi tȟósaŋ | | thiyópa tȟózi | | miméla šásaŋ |

7 🔊 Reading and writing Lakota **kh**, **ph** and **th** (aspirated stops).

Reading and writing **kh**. Lakota **kh** sounds like the English **k** in **kite**.

kh

khéya

khe khe khe

khi khi

khu khu

khiŋ khiŋ

Reading and writing **ph**. Lakota **ph** sounds like the English **p** in **pool**.

ph

pheží

phe phe phe

phi phi

phu phu

phiŋ phiŋ

Reading and writing **th**. Lakota **th** sounds like the English **t** in **take**.

the   the   the

thi thi

thu thu

thiŋ thiŋ

8 **What do you hear? Listen and point.**

khe	khi	khu	khiŋ
phe	phi	phu	phiŋ
the	thi	thu	thiŋ

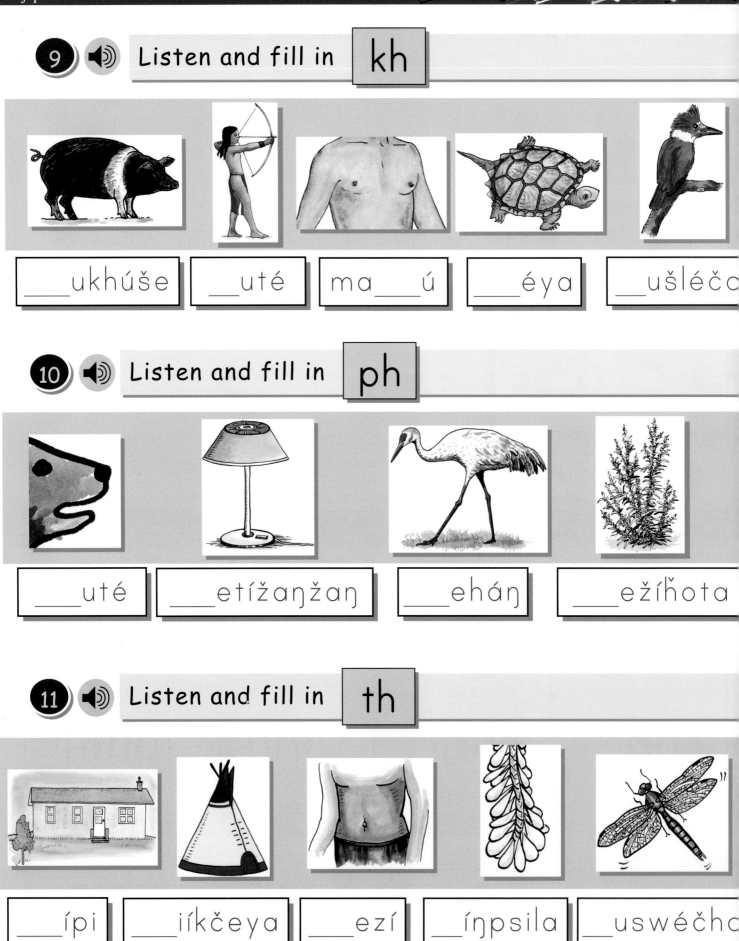

9 Listen and fill in **kh**

___ukhúše __uté ma___ú ___éya __ušléč[c]

10 Listen and fill in **ph**

___uté ___etížaŋžaŋ ___eháŋ ___ežíȟota

11 Listen and fill in **th**

___ípi __iíkčeya __ezí __íŋpsila __uswéčh[c]

12

Color in all the original colors and the new mixed color.
Fill in the proper mixed color name.

zí   šá

_____

tȟó   šá

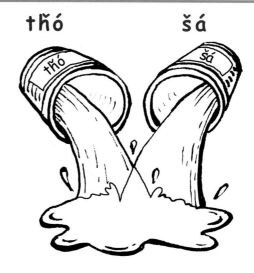

_____

tȟó   sáŋ

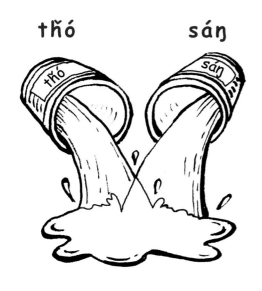

_____

šá   sáŋ

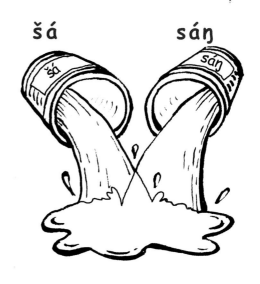

_____

tȟó   sápa

_____

tȟó   zí

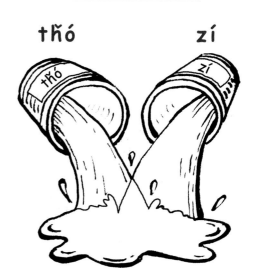

_____

13 **"The dog is black."** Read Bob's statements below.

Lé šúŋka.

Šúŋka kiŋ sápe.

> Lé <u>šúŋka</u>. = This <u>is a dog</u>.
>
> Šúŋka kiŋ <u>sápe</u>. = The dog <u>is black</u>.

Read what Bob says about the dog. Fill in the missing words in the sentences below:

This <u>is a book</u>.	Lé <u>wówapi</u>.
The book <u>is blue</u>.	Wówapi _____ <u>tȟó</u>.

This <u>is a cat</u>.	Lé _____.
The cat <u>is white</u>.	Igmú kiŋ _____.

14 **"This chair is red."** Match the sentences with the pictures.

> Oákaŋke kiŋ lé šá.
>
> Kimímela kiŋ lé šá.
>
> Šúŋka kiŋ lé ǧí.
>
> Igmú kiŋ lé ǧí.
>
> Wíčazo kiŋ lé zíša.
>
> Ziŋtkála kiŋ lé tȟó.
>
> Šúŋka kiŋ lé sápe.
>
> Šúŋkawakȟáŋ kiŋ lé zí.

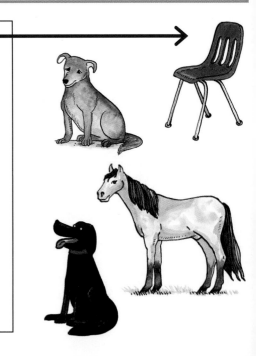

15 "This dog is NOT white." Circle the correct sentence.

Šúŋka kiŋ lé **ská**. (Šúŋka kiŋ lé **ská šni**.)

(Ziŋtkála kiŋ lé **sápe**.) Ziŋtkála kiŋ lé **sápe šni**.

Šúŋkawakȟáŋ kiŋ lé **šá**. Šúŋkawakȟáŋ kiŋ lé **šá šni**.

Pȟahíŋ kiŋ lé **tȟózi**. Pȟahíŋ kiŋ lé **tȟózi šni**.

Khukhúše kiŋ lé **šásaŋ**. Khukhúše kiŋ lé **šásaŋ šni**.

Ptegléška kiŋ lé **ȟóte**. Ptegléška kiŋ lé **ȟóte šni**.

Maǧá kiŋ lé **tȟósapa**. Maǧá kiŋ lé **tȟósape šni**.

Thuswéčha kiŋ lé **šá**. Thuswéčha kiŋ lé **šá šni**.

Waŋblí kiŋ lé **tȟósaŋ**. Waŋblí kiŋ lé **tȟósaŋ šni**.

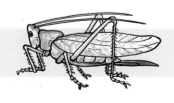

Gnugnúška kiŋ lé **tȟózi**. Gnugnúška kiŋ lé **tȟózi šni**.

Read the two dialogs between Bob and Lisa.

Wówapi kiŋ **lé oówa tókča** hwo?

Hé **tȟó**.

Šúŋka kiŋ **lé híŋ tókča** he?

Hé **sápe**.

FUR or COLOR? Compare the two dialogs above. Then fill in **oówa** (color) or **híŋ** (fur/hair) below:

Wíyatke kiŋ _____ tókča hwo/he?

Wíyatke kiŋ šá.

Igmú kiŋ _____ tókča hwo/he?

Igmú kiŋ ská.

Hint: **tókča** means 'what' or 'how'.
When talking about things we can also ask:
Wíyuŋpi tókča hwo/he? – What paint?

17 Fur or color? Fill in **híŋ** or **oówa** to ask the right question. Then write the answer.

Wówapi kiŋ lé ___oówa___ tókča hwo/he? __Lé tȟó.__

Šúŋka kiŋ lé ___híŋ___ tókča hwo/he? __Lé ǧí.__

Šúŋkawakȟáŋ kiŋ lé _____ tókča hwo/he? _____

Wíčazo kiŋ lé _____ tókča hwo/he? _____

Khukhúše kiŋ lé _____ tókča hwo/he? _____

Ptegléška kiŋ lé _____ tókča hwo/he? _____

Wagmíza kiŋ lé _____ tókča hwo/he? _____

Oákaŋke kiŋ lé _____ tókča hwo/he? _____

Šuŋǧíla kiŋ lé _____ tókča hwo/he? _____

Zičá kiŋ lé _____ tókča hwo/he? _____

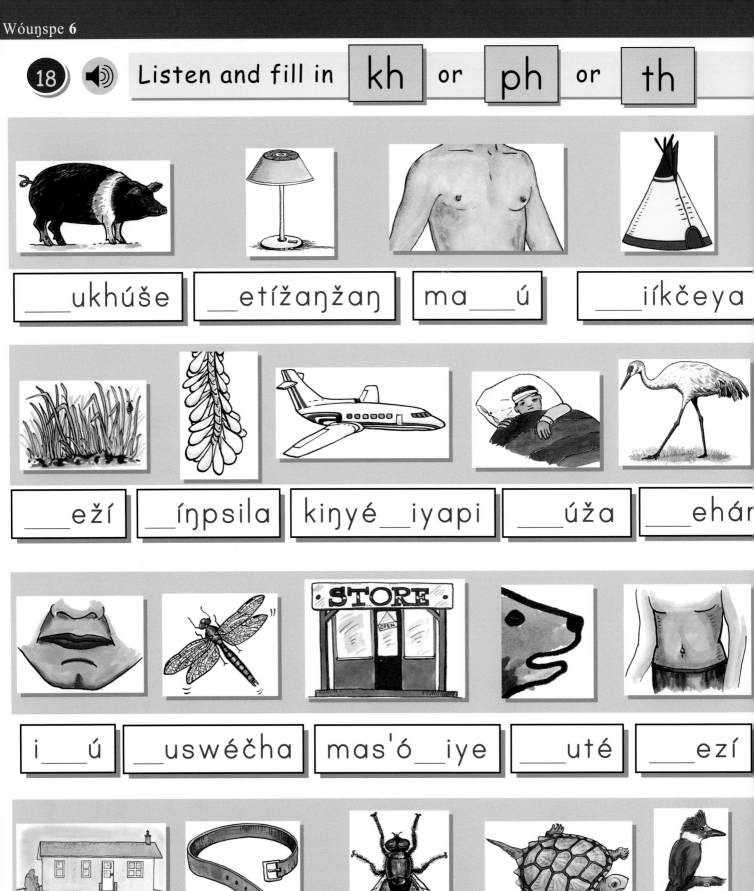

18 🔊 Listen and fill in **kh** or **ph** or **th**

___ukhúše   ___etížaŋžaŋ   ma___ú   ___iíkčeya

___eží   ___íŋpsila   kiŋyé___iyapi   ___úža   ___ehán

i___ú   ___uswéčha   mas'ó___iye   ___uté   ___ezí

___ípi   i___íyaka   ___eȟmúǧa   ___éya   ___ušléč

19 Circle the correct sentence.

Wíyatke kiŋ **lé** zíša.   Wíyatke kiŋ **hé** zíša.

Šúŋka kiŋ **lé** ǧí.   Šúŋka kiŋ **hé** ǧí.

Kimímela kiŋ **lé** šá.   Kimímela kiŋ **hé** šá.

Wíčazo kiŋ **lé** sápe.   Wíčazo kiŋ **hé** sápe.

20 What is the teacher asking Bob and Lisa to do?

21 What are the differences between the two pictures? List them on the next page.

22 Fill in the proper colors to discover the hidden picture on the right.

Picture A:	Picture B:
šúŋka **sápe**	šúŋka **ská**
igmú	igmú
thiyópa	thiyópa
wíyatke	wíyatke
oákaŋke	oákaŋke
wówapi	wówapi
šúŋkawakȟáŋ	šúŋkawakȟáŋ
čhaŋbláska	čhaŋbláska
akáŋwowapi	akáŋwowapi
tȟaspáŋ	tȟaspáŋ
wakšíča	wakšíča
wíčazo	wíčazo
wóžuha	wóžuha

23 Odd one out. Cross out the word that doesn't belong in each line.

napčíyuŋka	~~šúŋka~~	šaglóǧaŋ	šakówiŋ
gnašká	wakšíča	wóžuha	oákaŋke
pispíza	čhápa	kimímela	waŋží
maká	tópa	šákpe	yámni
tȟó	zí	núŋpa	šá
ǧí	tȟaspáŋ	zíškopa	kȟáŋta
akáŋwowapi	čhaŋbláska	wíčazo	tȟósapa

7 Lená mitȟáwa.   These are mine.

Listen to Lisa describing her clothes. Point to each object as it is named. Use the colors to help you.
Repeat the pointing exercise with Bob's clothes.

Lená mitȟáwa:

ógle

čhuwígnaka

huŋyákȟuŋ

iphíyaka

nitéhepi

uŋzóǧe

háŋpa

ógle

ógle šókela

uŋzóǧe

huŋyákȟuŋ

iphíyaka

napíŋkpa

wapȟóštaŋ

háŋpa

Lená mitȟáwa:

2 Match the words with the pictures. Use the colors to help you.

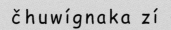
čhuwígnaka zí

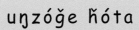
uŋzóǧe ȟóta

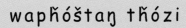
wapȟóštaŋ tȟózi

ógle ská

nitéhepi tȟósaŋ

iphíyaka sápe

napíŋkpa ǧí

háŋpa tȟóša

ógle-zigzíča zíša

ógle-šókela tȟó

huŋyákȟuŋ sáŋ

3 🔊 Lakota **g** sounds like the English **g** in **goal**. It is always followed by a consonant.

G g

gnaška

gla   gla gla

gma   gma

gna   gna

gwa   gwa

4 🔊 Listen and repeat Lakota **ǧ**.
It is always followed by a vowel.

Ǧ ǧ

ǧí

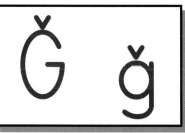

ǧa   ǧa ǧa

ǧe   ǧe

ǧi   ǧi

ǧo   ǧo

ǧu   ǧu

ǧaŋ   ǧaŋ

ǧiŋ   ǧiŋ

ǧuŋ   ǧuŋ

⑤ 🔊 **Listen and fill in** [**g**] **or** [**ǧ**]

__naška   __í   wa__lékšuŋ   a__úyapi   núŋ__e

ŋzó__e   šuŋ__íla   wa__míza   ťhašíya_nuŋpa   ho_áŋ

wá_ačhaŋ   i__mú   čhuwí_naka   kȟaŋ_í   ma_áksiča

wičhíte_le_a   ma__á   ó_le   wá_lotapi   čháŋčhe_a

6 Match the pictures that begin with the same letter.

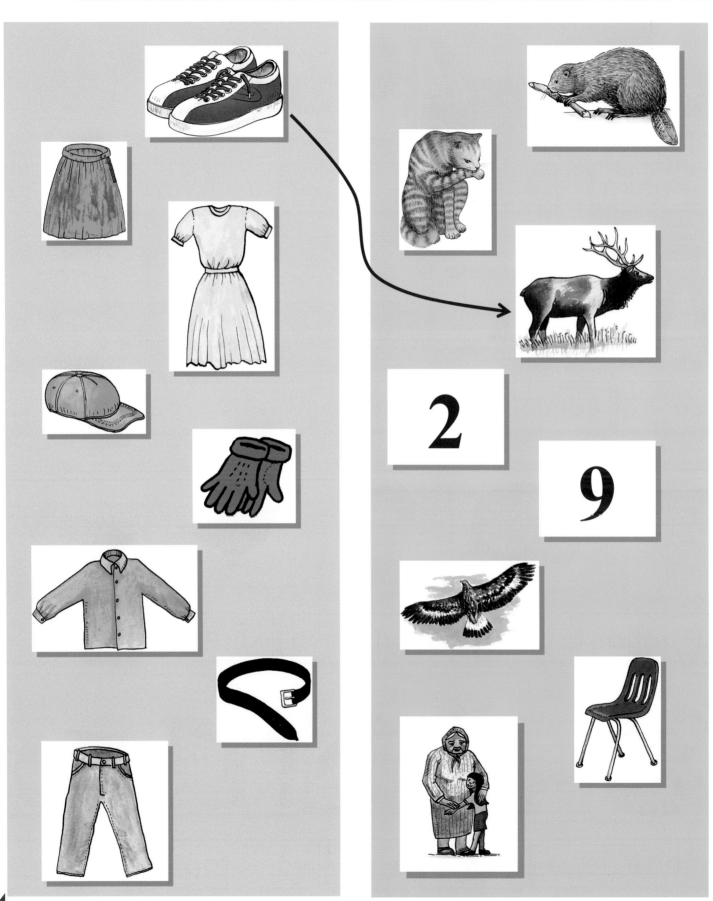

7 Can you find all the words for clothes?

g	n	i	t	é	h	e	p	i	n	th
kȟ	aŋ	s	ú	kh	u	t	e	čh	a	i
aŋ	o	š	t	é	g	l	n	u	w	y
t	h	uŋ	y	á	kȟ	uŋ	a	w	á	ó
á	t	a	n	a	t	z	p	í	ȟ	g
s	uŋ	i	a	pȟ	aŋ	ó	íŋ	g	h	n
u	š	í	p	a	z	ǧ	k	n	áŋ	a
iŋ	ǧ	aŋ	ó	g	l	e	p	a	p	k
k	iŋ	n	i	ph	í	y	a	k	a	a
p	w	a	pȟ	ó	š	t	aŋ	a	m	ȟ

8 Odd one out. Cross out the word in each row that does not belong.

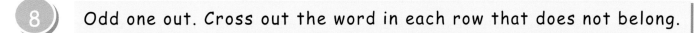

napčíyuŋka	~~tȟatȟáŋka~~	šaglóǧaŋ	šakówiŋ
maká	wakšíča	wíčazo	oákaŋke
iphíyake	šakówiŋ	háŋpa	ógle
khéya	huŋyákȟuŋ	napíŋkpa	wapȟóštaŋ
maká	tópa	šákpe	yámni
tȟósaŋ	tȟózi	zíša	čhuwígnaka
ǧí	tȟaspáŋ	zíškopa	kȟáŋta

9 True or false? Circle **háŋ** or **hiyá**.

Lé wapȟóštaŋ héčha.   Háŋ   Hiyá

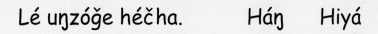

Lé uŋzóǧe héčha.   Háŋ   Hiyá

Lé iphíyaka héčha.   Háŋ   Hiyá

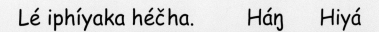

Lé ógle šókela héčha.   Háŋ   Hiyá

"My shirt is yellow."

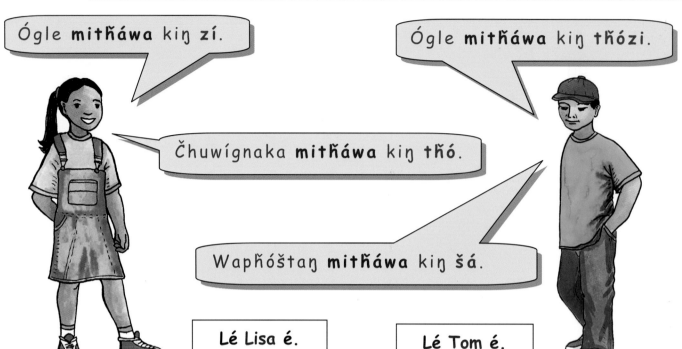

Ógle **mitȟáwa** kiŋ **zí**.

Ógle **mitȟáwa** kiŋ **tȟózi**.

Čhuwígnaka **mitȟáwa** kiŋ **tȟó**.

Wapȟóštaŋ **mitȟáwa** kiŋ **šá**.

Lé Lisa é.

Lé Tom é.

Look at the children above. Can you guess what they are saying?
If so, match the words as in the example.

| Ógle **mitȟáwa** | <u>My</u> <u>shirt</u>. | | Háŋpa **mitȟáwa** | <u>My</u> <u>shoes</u>. |

Fill in the missing words:

Ógle <u>mitȟáwa</u> kiŋ zí.	<u>My</u> shirt is yellow.
_____ mitȟáwa kiŋ šá.	My <u>hat</u> is red.
Nitéhepi _____ kiŋ zí.	<u>My</u> skirt is yellow.
Iphíyake mitȟáwa kiŋ ____.	My belt <u>is</u> <u>black</u>.

Notice that in Lakota we use **kiŋ** (**the**) in these sentences.
Can you say sentences like these about your own clothes?

11 Point at your clothes and say sentences like this:
Lé ógle mitȟáwa. – This is my shirt.

12 What color are your things? Color the pictures and finish the sentence about them. Find a partner and repeat the question with each of the objects.

Ógle **nitȟáwa** kiŋ oówa tókča he?

Ógle mitȟáwa kiŋ šá.

1. Ógle mitȟáwa kiŋ

2. Uŋzóǧe mitȟáwa kiŋ

3. Nitéhepi mitȟáwa kiŋ

4. Wapȟóštaŋ mitȟáwa kiŋ

5. Háŋpa mitȟáwa kiŋ

6. Iphíyaka mitȟáwa kiŋ

7. Huŋyákȟuŋ mitȟáwa kiŋ

8. Čhuwígnaka mitȟáwa kiŋ

13 | **Who is who?** Read about their clothes to find out their names.

Paul ógle <u>tȟáwa</u> kiŋ tȟó
na háŋpa <u>tȟáwa</u> kiŋ tȟotȟó
na uŋzóǧe <u>tȟáwa</u> kiŋ sápe.

Ivan uŋzóǧe tȟáwa kiŋ tȟózi
na ógle tȟáwa kiŋ tȟóša
na háŋpa tȟáwa kiŋ sapsápe.

Lé _____ é.

Lé _____ é.

Martina uŋzóǧe tȟáwa kiŋ tȟó,
ógle tȟáwa kiŋ zí
na háŋpa tȟáwa kiŋ tȟotȟó.

Lucy nitéhepi tȟáwa kiŋ tȟó,
ógle tȟáwa kiŋ šá
na háŋpa tȟáwa kiŋ šašá.

Lé _____ é.

Lé ___Paul___ é.

Tom ógle tȟáwa kiŋ tȟózi
na wapȟóštaŋ tȟáwa kiŋ šá
na uŋzóǧe tȟáwa kiŋ tȟó.

Dana čhuwígnaka tȟáwa kiŋ
šá, háŋpa tȟáwa kiŋ tȟotȟó.

Lé _____ é.

Lé _____ é.

14 His shirt is blue. – **Ógle tȟáwa kiŋ tȟó.**

Did you read about the children's clothes on the previous page?
Try to match the words:

| ógle tȟáwa | his/her shirt | | uŋzóǧe tȟáwa | his/her pants |

Fill in the missing word:

| _____ tȟáwa | his/her **gloves** |
| iphíyake _____ | **his/her** belt |

Ógle tȟáwa kiŋ _____ .

His shirt is black.

---

15 **Paul's shirt is blue. – Paul ógle tȟáwa kiŋ tȟó.**
Fill in the proper color using the pictures on the left-hand page.
Then write the English translation.

Paul ógle tȟáwa kiŋ _____**tȟó**_____.   Paul's shirt is blue.

Tom wapȟóštaŋ tȟáwa kiŋ _____.   _____

Ivan uŋzóǧe tȟáwa kiŋ _____.   _____

Lucy ógle tȟáwa kiŋ _____.   _____

Martina háŋpa tȟáwa kiŋ _____.   _____

Dana čhuwígnaka tȟáwa kiŋ ____.   _____

---

16 True or false? Read the sentences and circle **háŋ** or **hiyá**.

Paul wapȟóštaŋ tȟáwa kiŋ sápe.	(Háŋ)	Hiyá
Lucy ógle tȟáwa kiŋ tȟó.	Háŋ	Hiyá
Dana háŋpa tȟáwa kiŋ šašá.	Háŋ	Hiyá
Tom wapȟóštaŋ tȟáwa kiŋ šá.	Háŋ	Hiyá
Martina ógle tȟáwa kiŋ tȟózi.	Háŋ	Hiyá
Ivan uŋzóǧe tȟáwa kiŋ sápe.	Háŋ	Hiyá

17 Mary's and Lucy's clothes got mixed up. Read how Mary and Lucy describe their clothes and then mark Mary's clothes with **M** and Lucy's with **L**.

Mary

Uŋzóǧe mitȟáwa kiŋ ȟóte.
Čhuwígnaka mitȟáwa kiŋ tȟó.
Huŋyákȟuŋ mitȟáwa kiŋ tȟózi.
Ógle zigzíča mitȟáwa kiŋ tȟóša.
Háŋpa mitȟáwa kiŋ šašá.
Iphíyaka mitȟáwa kiŋ ǧí.
Wapȟóštaŋ mitȟáwa kiŋ šá.
Nitéhepi mitȟáwa kiŋ tȟó.

L

M

Uŋzóǧe mitȟáwa kiŋ tȟó.
Čhuwígnaka mitȟáwa kiŋ šá.
Huŋyákȟuŋ mitȟáwa kiŋ tȟotȟó.
Ógle zigzíča mitȟáwa kiŋ tȟósaŋ.
Háŋpa mitȟáwa kiŋ ǧiǧí.
Iphíyaka mitȟáwa kiŋ sápe.
Wapȟóštaŋ mitȟáwa kiŋ tȟózi.
Nitéhepi mitȟáwa kiŋ zí.

Lucy

18 True or false? Circle háŋ or hiyá.

Wapȟóštaŋ kiŋ lé tȟózi.   Háŋ   Hiyá

Uŋzóǧe kiŋ lé šá.   Háŋ   Hiyá

Nitéhepi kiŋ lé zí.   Háŋ   Hiyá

Ógle šókela kiŋ lé tȟó.   Háŋ   Hiyá

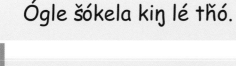

Háŋpa kiŋ lená šašá.   Háŋ   Hiyá

Huŋyákȟuŋ kiŋ lená zizí.   Háŋ   Hiyá

Napíŋkpa kiŋ lená ǧiǧí.   Háŋ   Hiyá

19 What are they asking Bob and Lisa to do?

Nážiŋ yo!

Íyotaka ye!

8 Thiwáhe mitȟáwa kiŋ.   My family.

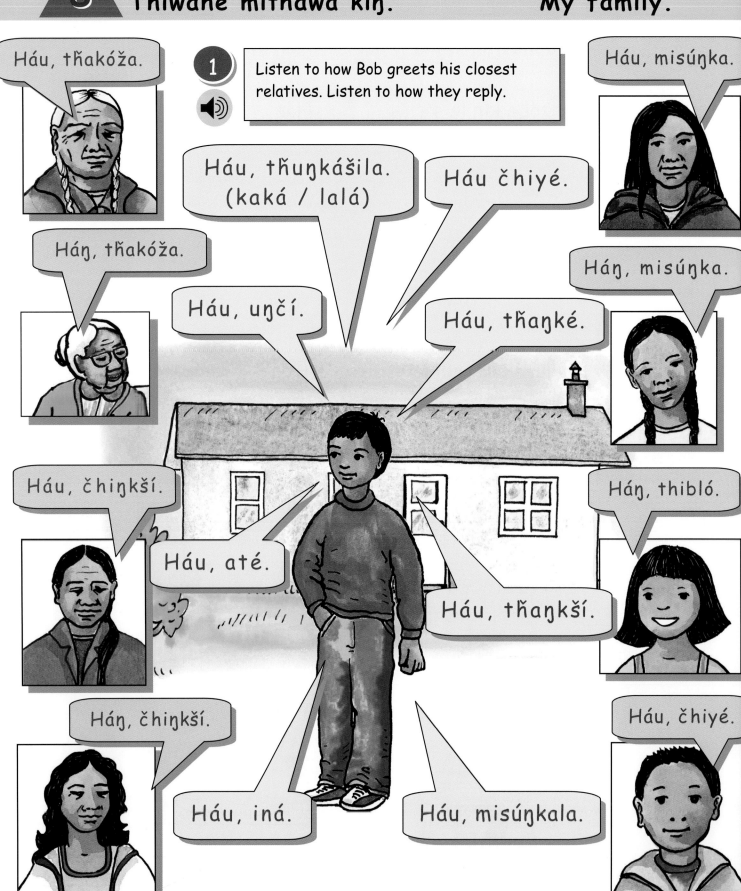

2 **Who is who?** Can you match the pictures with the words that Bob uses to address his relatives?

grandfather   grandmother   father   mother

čhiyé   uŋčí   tȟuŋkášila   tȟaŋkší   tȟaŋké   misúŋkala   iná   até

older brother   older sister   younger sister   younger brother

Listen to how Lisa greets her closest relatives. Listen to how they reply.

Háu, tȟakóža.

Háu, tȟaŋkší.

Háŋ, tȟuŋkášila.
(kaká / lalá)

Háŋ thibló.

Háŋ, tȟakóža.

Háŋ, mitȟáŋka.

Háŋ, uŋčí.

Háŋ, čhuwé.

Háu, čhuŋkší.

Háŋ, čhuwé.

Háŋ, até.

Háŋ, mitȟáŋkala.

Háŋ, čhuŋkší.

Háu, tȟaŋké.

Háŋ, iná.

Háŋ, misúŋkala.

4

Who is who? Can you match the pictures with the words that Lisa uses to address her relatives?

grandfather   grandmother   father   mother

čhuwé   até   tȟuŋkášila   mitȟáŋkala   thibló   misúŋkala   iná   uŋčí

older brother   older sister   younger sister   younger brother

Lakota **l**, **m**, **n** sound very similar to **l**, **m**, **n** in English. Listen, repeat and then write.

L l

l̲owáŋ

la la la la
le le le
li li li
lo lo lo
lu lu lu

M m

m̲atȟó

ma ma ma ma
me me me
mi mi mi
mo mo mo
mu mu mu

N n

n̲apé

na na na ma
ne ne ne
ni ni ni
no no no
nu nu nu

Draw a picture of your family. Write the Lakota kinship word you use next to each person. If you can, write a sentence like this next to each person's name:
Atéwaye kiŋ Richard ečíyapi. – My father's name is Richard.

7 🔊 Listen and fill in | l | or | m | or | n |

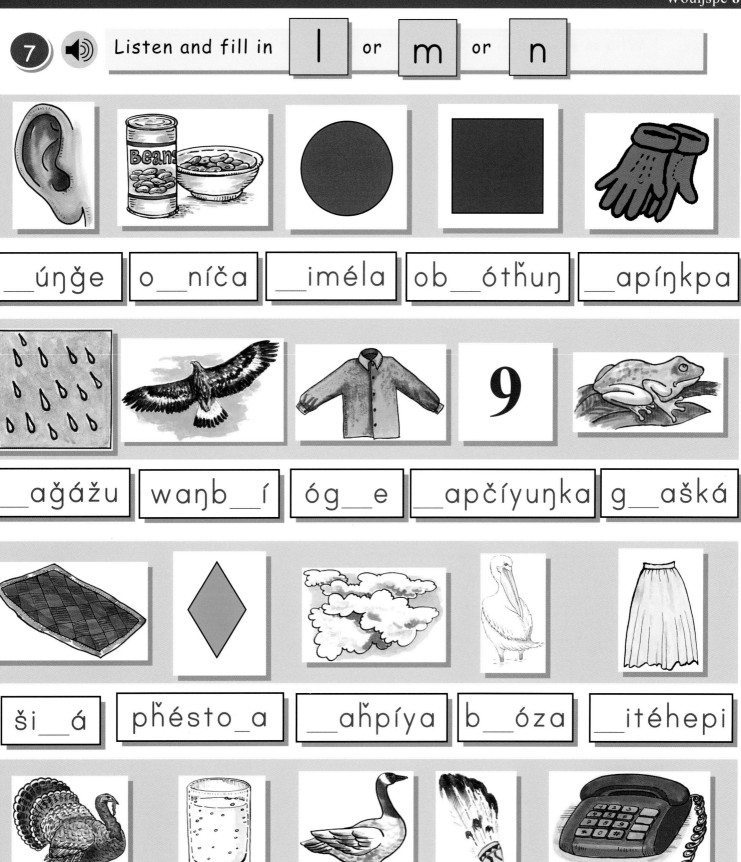

__úŋǧe   o__níča   __iméla   ob__ótȟuŋ   __apíŋkpa

__aǧážu   waŋb__í   óg__e   __apčíyuŋka   g__ašká

ši__á   pȟésto_a   __aȟpíya   b__óza   __itéhepi

wag__ékšuŋ   __ní   __aǧá   íča__u   o__ás'apȟe

8

Who is who? Bob is telling us the names of his brothers and sisters. Fill in their names next to the pictures below.

Čhiyéwaye kiŋ RICK ečíyapi.

Tȟaŋkéwaye kiŋ BETTY ečíyapi.

Tȟaŋkšíwaye kiŋ ANN ečíyapi.

Suŋkáwaye kiŋ MATTHEW ečíyapi.

_____Rick_____ emáčiyapi.

_____ emáčiyapi.

_____ emáčiyapi.

_____ emáčiyapi.

Lé _____ é.   Lé _____ é.   Lé _____ é.   Lé _Rick_ é.

Notice how Bob says "**My older brother**" – Čhiyéwaye kiŋ.

9 **Who is who?** Lisa is telling us the names of her brothers and sisters. Fill in their names next to the pictures below.

Thiblówaye kiŋ JOHN ečíyapi.

Čhuwéwaye kiŋ SHAWNA ečíyapi.

Tȟaŋkáwaye kiŋ JESSICA ečíyapi.

Suŋkáwaye kiŋ JAMES ečíyapi.

_____ emáčiyapi.

_____ emáčiyapi.

_____ emáčiyapi.

_____ emáčiyapi.

Lé _____ é.   Lé _____ é.   Lé _____ é.   Lé _____ é.

Fill in how Lisa says "**My** older brother" - Thibló_____.

10 Match the kinship words with the English translations.

boy's older brother   girl's older sister   boy's younger sister

father

čhuwé

tȟakóža

grandchild

iná

tȟaŋkší

čhiyé

uŋčí

mother

grandmother

até

čhiŋkší

younger brother

tȟuŋkášila

son

čhuŋkší

mitȟáŋka

grandfather

daughter

tȟaŋké

misúŋka

thibló

girl's younger sister

boy's older sister   girl's older brother

11 Draw a line from each kinship word to the picture that matches.

iná
até
tȟaŋké
čhuŋkší
thibló
uŋčí
čhiyé
mitȟáŋkala
čhuwé
čhiŋkší
tȟuŋkášila
tȟakóža
tȟaŋkší
misúŋkala

12 Match the kinship words with the "my .... " kinship words.

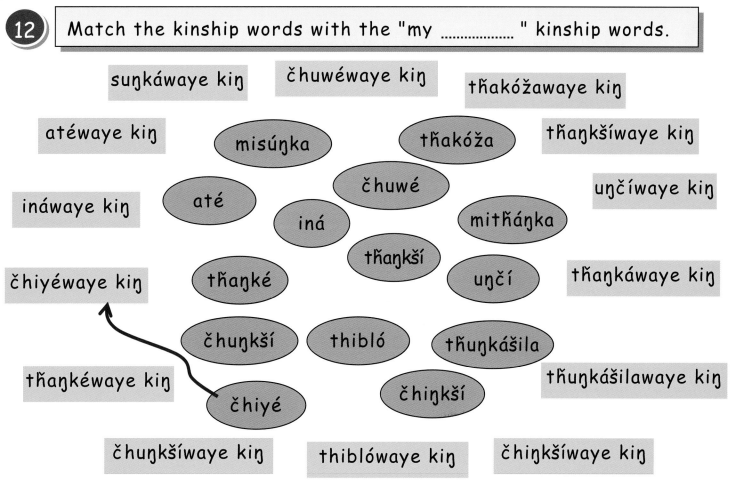

suŋkáwaye kiŋ

čhuwéwaye kiŋ

tȟakóžawaye kiŋ

atéwaye kiŋ

misúŋka

tȟakóža

tȟaŋkšíwaye kiŋ

čhuwé

uŋčíwaye kiŋ

ináwaye kiŋ

até

iná

mitȟáŋka

tȟaŋkší

čhiyéwaye kiŋ

tȟaŋké

uŋčí

tȟaŋkáwaye kiŋ

čhuŋkší

thibló

tȟuŋkášila

tȟaŋkéwaye kiŋ

čhiyé

čhiŋkší

tȟuŋkášilawaye kiŋ

čhuŋkšíwaye kiŋ

thiblówaye kiŋ

čhiŋkšíwaye kiŋ

13 Which of these kinship words are used **by a boy** and which **by a girl**? And which by both? Draw a line from Lisa and Bob to the words they use.

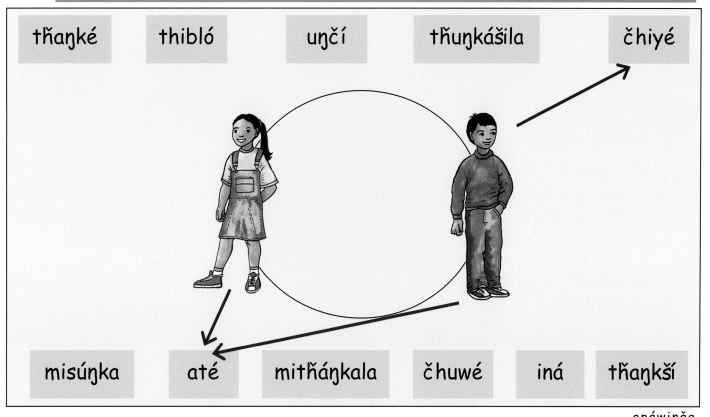

tȟaŋké   thibló   uŋčí   tȟuŋkášila   čhiyé

misúŋka   até   mitȟáŋkala   čhuwé   iná   tȟaŋkší

14 Can you find all the kinship words?

aŋ	p	í	y	u	l	z	a	t	é	g	y	a	b
k	a	g	čh	iŋ	k	š	í	y	u	h	e	n	i
s	k	a	n	a	p	uŋ	i	uŋ	k	á	h	e	l
aŋ	p	é	t	uŋ	g	čh	u	n	a	tȟ	aŋ	k	é
a	pȟ	é	y	o	č	a	aŋ	pȟ	a	s	ú	h	a
š	aŋ	tȟ	aŋ	k	š	í	ǧ	a	čh	a	kh	é	l
k	s	iŋ	t	é	ȟ	l	a	n	a	m	a	k	á
iŋ	k	tȟ	uŋ	k	á	š	i	l	a	e	tȟ	ó	ȟ
y	í	z	u	čh	é	y	a	tȟ	á	w	a	h	a
tȟ	a	h	á	u	w	í	m	i	tȟ	áŋ	k	a	o
áŋ	m	čh	a	w	é	w	a	n	á	h	ó	n	a
k	á	uŋ	tȟ	é	l	ph	i	á	n	u	ž	í	kh
i	y	k	a	th	i	b	l	ó	n	i	a	y	uŋ
tȟ	b	š	g	l	u	h	m	i	s	úŋ	k	a	š
á	n	í	y	aŋ	g	kȟ	ó	a	pȟ	á	z	í	l

tȟuŋkášila	uŋčí	até
iná	čhiyé	thibló
čhuwé	tȟaŋké	mitȟáŋka
misúŋka	čhiŋkší	čhuŋkší
tȟaŋkší	tȟakóža	

15 🔊 **Listen and fill in** ħ **or** ğ

   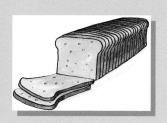 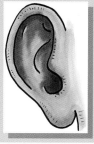

| uŋzó_e | _é | he_áka | a_úyapi | núŋ_e |

  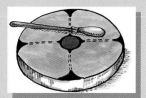  

| waná_ča | ho_áŋ | čháŋčhe_a | _oká | wá_ačhaŋ |

| šuŋ_íla | ma_ážu | ma_píya | kħaŋ_í | ma_áksiča |

| wičhítegle_a | ma_á | wa_pé | wičhá_pi | čhé__a |

9 Tȟaŋčháŋ. Body.

1 Read and listen to the words for body parts. Point to the words as you hear them.

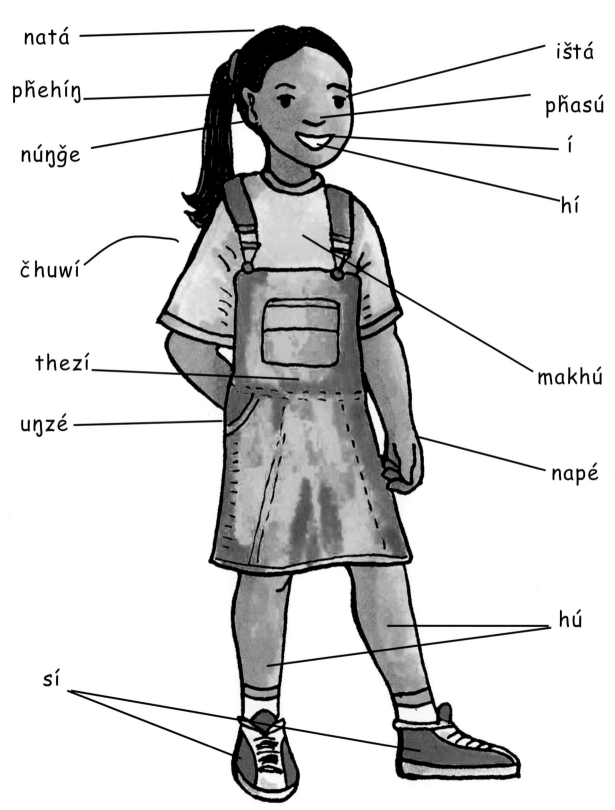

natá

pȟehíŋ

núŋǧe

čhuwí

thezí

uŋzé

ištá

pȟasú

í

hí

makhú

napé

hú

sí

2 Bob has a **šúŋka** named George. He knows all his body parts in Lakota. Listen and point to them as you hear them.

ištá — natá — nakpá — čhuwí — híŋ — siŋté — phuté — čheží — makhú — sí — uŋzé — hú — hí — í — thezí — sí

3 Compare the picture of the dog with the picture of the girl and decide what the words below mean. Then find out the English meaning of the other body parts.

HUMAN "two legged"	ANIMAL "four legged"
phuté upper lip	phuté snout
pȟehíŋ	híŋ
núŋǧe	nakpá
napé	siŋté

Lakota **b**, **w**, **y** sound the same as **b**, **w**, **y** in English. Practice writing them.

B b

<u>b</u>ébela

W w

<u>w</u>ičhíŋčala

Y y

3

<u>y</u>ámni

ba	ba	ba
be	be	be
bi	bi	bi
bo	bo	bo
bu	bu	bu

wa	wa	wa
we	we	we
wi	wi	wi
wo	wo	wo
wu	wu	wu
waŋ	waŋ	waŋ
wiŋ	wiŋ	wiŋ

ya	ya	ya
ye	ye	ye
yi	yi	yi
yo	yo	yo
yu	yu	yu
yaŋ	yaŋ	yaŋ
yiŋ	yiŋ	yiŋ
yuŋ	yuŋ	yuŋ

5 🔊 Listen and fill in **b** or **w** or **y**

__ígmuŋke   __ló   ičá__u   o__lótȟuŋ   __ičhíŋčala

__ámni   waŋ__lí   __agmíza   __ičháȟpi   wí__ukse

__áǧačhaŋ   wí__aka   __lóza   maȟpí__a   __ébela

__apȟóštaŋ   __lé   __aȟpé   wí__atke   __áglotapi

6 Lisa's **igmú**, Martha, is waiting for her to get home from school. Can you identify all her body parts?

natá

híŋ

nakpá

čhuwí

ištá

phuté

makhú

í

hí

thezí

čheží

uŋzé

hú

sí

siŋté

7 Can you find all the body parts?

i	kh	ú	s	i	čh	aŋ	t	é	l	a	h
g	í	b	i	š	t	á	n	áŋ	ǧ	m	iŋ
l	ž	u	h	á	p	p	tȟ	úŋ	ú	a	y
a	i	h	á	k	a	š	a	a	l	kh	é
e	s	iŋ	a	o	l	i	čh	aŋ	h	ú	t
ph	t	n	ú	s	iŋ	t	é	u	ȟ	ú	e
u	ó	n	n	úŋ	ǧ	e	ž	ú	w	aŋ	ž
t	ú	m	a	tȟ	n	ú	čh	e	ž	í	ȟ
é	pȟ	a	p	p	s	a	š	w	z	s	é
s	uŋ	z	é	a	s	a	w	e	l	t	čh
i	š	t	pȟ	á	tȟ	ú	th	á	ȟ	á	aŋ
čh	a	ž	p	e	š	a	k	a	t	o	k
áŋ	p	k	é	h	h	h	pȟ	a	s	e	p
i	e	t	s	í	kȟ	íŋ	n	úŋ	z	ȟ	é
čh	i	š	t	á	ȟ	e	h	iŋ	ǧ	a	k

Body parts from this unit:		Additional body parts (from Level 1):	
~~pȟasú~~	hú	čhaŋkpé	ihá
čheží	makhú	čhaŋté	ikhú
nakpá	napé	hiŋyéte	ištáȟehiŋ
pȟehíŋ	natá	istó	ité
híŋ	sí	išpá	nawáte
ištá	thezí	napsúkaza	osúŋ
núŋǧe	uŋzé	sičháŋ	pȟaȟté
phuté	hí	tȟahú	tȟapȟúŋ
čhuwí	siŋté	čhekpá	

8 🔊 Review. Listen and fill in [S] or [Š]

_uŋǧíla   _iŋté   oí_e yámni   pȟa_ú   waglék_uŋ

pȟatká_a   itȟúŋka_aŋ   huŋ_ká   tȟa_náheča

9 🔊 Review. Listen and fill in [z] or [ž]

wa_í   wó_api   wagmí_a   upí_ata   bló__a

tȟa_úška   _ičá   phetí_aŋ_aŋ   waŋ_í   _u_éča

10 Bob's tȟuŋkášila is a traditional dancer. Can you identify all his body parts?

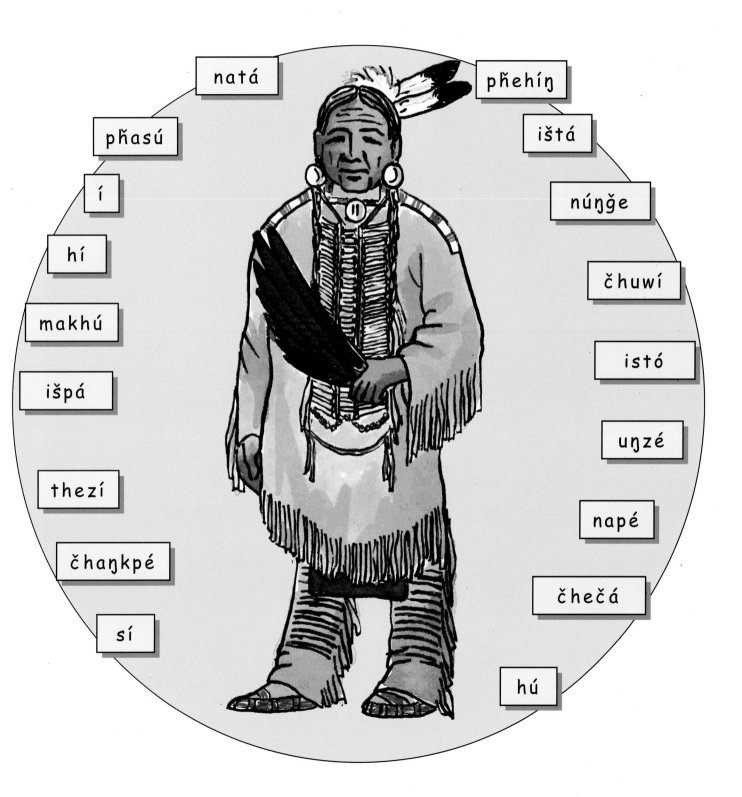

natá

pȟehíŋ

pȟasú

ištá

í

núŋǧe

hí

čhuwí

makhú

istó

išpá

uŋzé

thezí

napé

čhaŋkpé

čhečá

sí

hú

11 Match the words for the clothes with the pictures. Then match them with the body parts they cover.

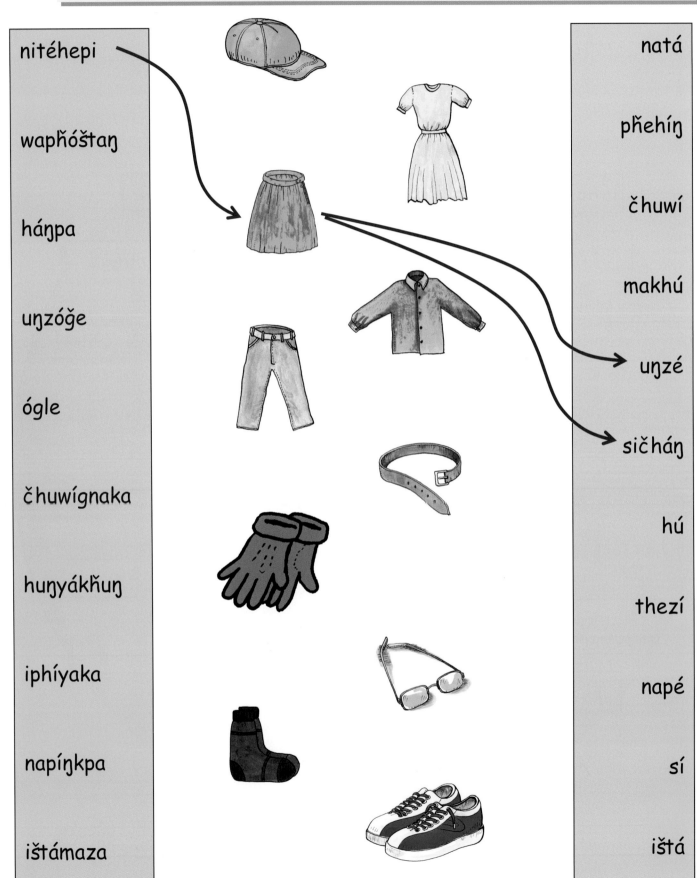

nitéhepi

wapȟóštaŋ

háŋpa

uŋzóǧe

ógle

čhuwígnaka

huŋyákȟuŋ

iphíyaka

napíŋkpa

ištámaza

natá

pȟehíŋ

čhuwí

makhú

uŋzé

sičháŋ

hú

thezí

napé

sí

ištá

12 Count the body parts of Bob's **šúŋka** (dog). Match the words for body parts with a number.
(Hint: **óta** means '**many**' or '**much**'.)

| natá | čhuwí | makhú | sí | thezí | hú | ištá | čhెží | hí | í | pȟasú | núŋǧe | híŋ |

| waŋží | tópa | óta | núŋpa |

13 **Hú tóna?**
Living beings come in all shapes and sizes. Some have few legs, some have many. Match the living beings with the number of legs they have. (Hint: **waníče** means 'To have none'.)

šúŋkawakȟáŋ		hokšíla
gnugnúška	núŋpa	igmú
siŋtéȟla		tȟažúška
hoǧáŋ	tópa	šúŋka
waŋblí	šákpe	wičhíŋčala
matȟó	šaglóǧaŋ	kimímela
čhapȟúŋka	waníče	iktómi

10 Táku tókȟuŋpi hwo/he?   What are they doing?

1

Animals can do many things. Look at the animals below. See if you can tell what they are doing. Listen and point to the animals you hear.

nážiŋ

máni

psíče

nuŋwé

yuŋké

yaŋké

íŋyaŋke

ištíŋme

2 Use the left-hand page to see what the animals are doing. Complete the sentences using the verbs. Then listen to the CD again (Exercise 1) to find out if you were right.

Tȟatȟáŋka kiŋ lé ___náźiŋ___.   psíče

Niǧésaŋla kiŋ lé _____.   ištíŋme

Matȟó kiŋ lé _____.   yaŋké

Igmú kiŋ lé _____.   íŋyaŋke

Šúŋka kiŋ lé _____.   náźiŋ

Čhápa kiŋ lé _____.   yuŋké

Maštíŋska kiŋ lé _____.   nuŋwé

Šúŋkawákȟaŋ kiŋ lé _____.   máni

3 Find a partner. Repeat Bob and Lisa's dialog – ask what each of the animals is doing.

Tȟatȟáŋka kiŋ lé **táku tókȟuŋ hwo?**

Náźiŋ.

4

These animals are doing different things. Read the questions below and circle the correct answers.

Pispíza kiŋ lé **nážiŋ** he?	(Háŋ, nážiŋ.)	Hiyá, nážiŋ šni.
Igmú kiŋ lé **íŋyaŋka** he?	Háŋ, íŋyaŋke.	(Hiyá, íŋyaŋke šni.)
Šúŋkawakȟáŋ kiŋ lé **máni** he?	Háŋ, máni.	Hiyá, máni šni.
Matȟó kiŋ lé **psíča** he?	Háŋ, psíče.	Hiyá, psíče šni.
Šúŋka kiŋ lé **yaŋká** he?	Háŋ, yaŋké.	Hiyá, yaŋké šni.
Tȟatȟáŋka kiŋ lé **yuŋká** he?	Háŋ, yuŋké.	Hiyá, yuŋké šni.
Niǧésaŋla kiŋ lé **nuŋwáŋ** he?	Háŋ, nuŋwé.	Hiyá, nuŋwé šni.
Maštíŋska kiŋ lé **ištíŋma** he?	Háŋ, ištíŋme.	Hiyá, ištíŋme šni.

5 The final **a** of some of the action words (verbs) changes to **e**. Can you tell when this happens?

<u>Igmú</u> kiŋ lé **íŋyaŋka** he?	Háŋ, íŋyaŋk**e**.	Hiyá, íŋyaŋk**e** šni.
<u>Matȟó</u> kiŋ lé **psíča** he?	Háŋ, psíč**e**.	Hiyá, psíč**e** šni.
<u>Šúŋka</u> kiŋ lé **yaŋká** he?	Háŋ, yaŋké.	Hiyá, yaŋké šni.
<u>Tȟatȟáŋka</u> kiŋ lé **yuŋká** he?	Háŋ, yuŋké.	Hiyá, yuŋké šni.
<u>Niǧésaŋla</u> kiŋ lé **nuŋwáŋ** he?	Háŋ, nuŋwé.	Hiyá, nuŋwé šni.
<u>Maštíŋska</u> kiŋ lé **ištíŋma** he?	Háŋ, ištíŋm**e**.	Hiyá, ištíŋm**e** šni.
<u>Pispíza</u> kiŋ lé **nážiŋ** he?	Háŋ, nážiŋ.	Hiyá, nážiŋ šni.
<u>Šúŋkawakȟáŋ</u> kiŋ lé **máni** he?	Háŋ, máni.	Hiyá, máni šni.

6 Find a partner and repeat the dialog using the animals on the left-hand page.

7 Reading and writing č', k', p', t'.

Č' č'

č'ó

č'a č'e č'i č'o č'u

K' k'

k'á

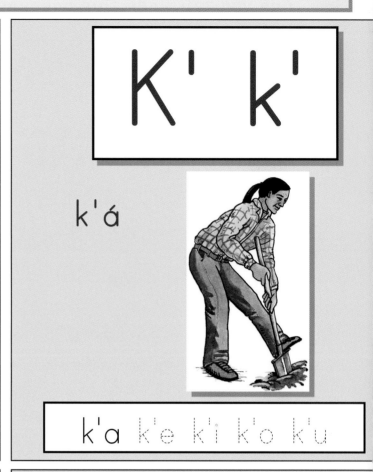

k'a k'e k'i k'o k'u

P' p'

p'ó

p'a p'e p'i p'o p'u

T' t'

t'á

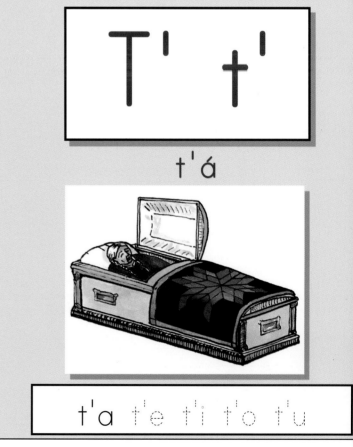

t'a t'e t'i t'o t'u

8   Glottal stop. Listen and point at the letter you hear.

Glottal stop is a Lakota sound we know from English as well. We say it in uh-oh or in kitten.
In Lakota it often follows ȟ, s and š, and we write it as an apostrophe: ȟ', s', š'
It is also part of the ejective stops we just learned: č', k', p', t'

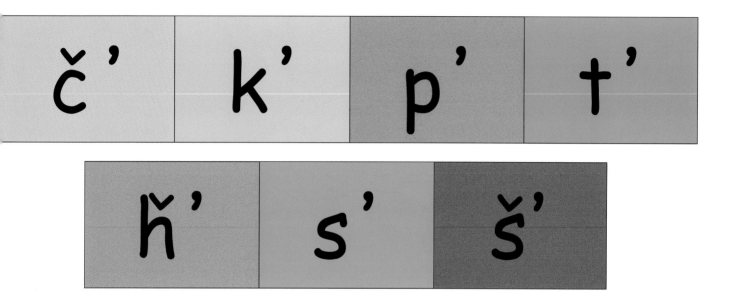

č' | k' | p' | t'

ȟ' | s' | š'

Listen again and fill in the missing letter.

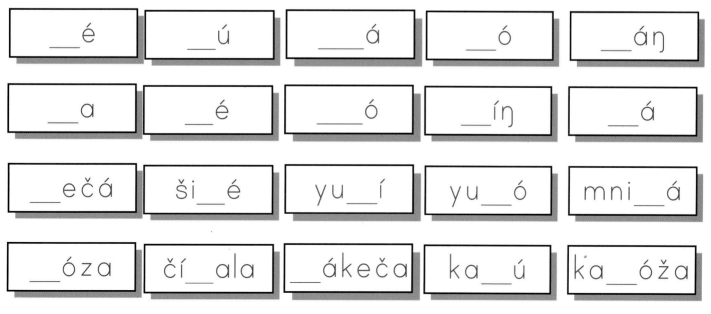

| __é | __ú | __á | __ó | __áŋ |

| __a | __é | __ó | __íŋ | __á |

| __ečá | ši__é | yu__í | yu__ó | mni__á |

| __óza | čí__ala | __ákeča | ka__ú | ka__óža |

9 Each mouse is doing something different and wearing a different colored suit. Use the picture and the verbs to complete the sentences below.

Itȟúŋkala šá kiŋ _____nážiŋ_____ ←   psíče

Itȟúŋkala zí kiŋ _____   ištíŋme

Itȟúŋkala tȟó kiŋ _____   yaŋké

Itȟúŋkala sápa kiŋ _____   íŋyaŋke

Itȟúŋkala tȟózi kiŋ _____   nážiŋ

Itȟúŋkala tȟóša kiŋ _____   yuŋké

Itȟúŋkala ǧí kiŋ _____   nuŋwé

Itȟúŋkala ská kiŋ _____   máni

10 Review. Fill in | č | or | čh |

  **10**

| __aŋháŋpi | __aŋkú | wik__émna | __apȟúŋka | i__ábu |

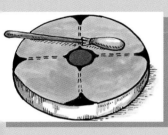    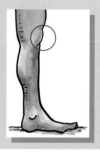

| __áŋčheǧa | uŋk__éla | tȟáȟ__a | zi__á | __aŋkpé |

| wanáȟ__a | wi__ítegleǧa | he__á | omní__a | wakší__a |

| waší__u | __aŋté | uŋ__í | uŋk__épagmigma | __áŋ |

Bob says, **"I am standing."** The other children are describing what they are doing. Listen and repeat what they say.

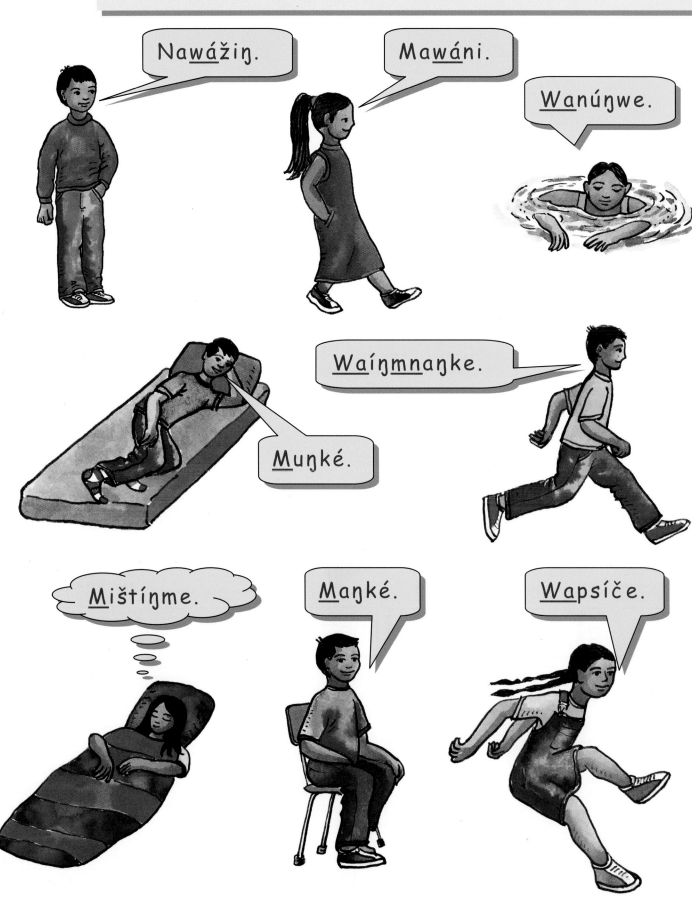

12 The word nawážiŋ means "I stand", nážiŋ means "he/she stands". Can you match the other "I" words with the "he/she" word"?

na<u>w</u>ážiŋ	nážiŋ	psíče
ma<u>w</u>áni		ištíŋme
<u>w</u>apsíče		yaŋké
<u>w</u>anúŋwe		íŋyaŋke
<u>m</u>aŋké		nážiŋ
<u>m</u>uŋké		yuŋké
<u>m</u>ištíŋme		nuŋwé
<u>w</u>aíŋmnaŋke		máni

13 Work in pairs. One of you acts out an activity, the other one says the proper verb. Then switch around.

Máni.

11 Nitáku hwo/he?

What are you?

wakȟáŋheža   **tȟéča kiŋ**

hokšíla   wičhíŋčala   kȟoškálaka   wikȟóškalaka

wičháȟčala   winúȟčala   wičháša   wíŋyaŋ

wakáŋ kiŋ   **tȟáŋka kiŋ**

2   The youngest dancer says: **"I am a Lakota boy"**. What do the others say? Listen and then say what you are.

Lakȟóta kȟo**má**škalaka.

Lakȟóta wi**má**čhiŋčala.

Lakȟóta wi**má**kȟoškalaka.

Lakȟóta ho**má**kšila.

wakȟáŋheža

tȟéča kiŋ

wakȟáŋ kiŋ

tȟáŋka kiŋ

Lakȟóta wi**má**čhaȟčala.

Lakȟóta wi**má**čhaša.

Lakȟóta wi**má**nuȟčala.

Lakȟóta wiŋ**má**yaŋ.

3 Match the pictures with the words for people.

kȟoškálaka   wičhíŋčala   hokšíla   wičháȟčala   wikȟóškalaka   wičháša   wíŋyaŋ   winúȟčala

| James | Jessica | Rick | Betty | Phil | Mary | Cecilia | Peter |

tȟéča kiŋ   wakȟáŋheža   wakáŋ kiŋ   tȟáŋka kiŋ

4 What are the names of the people above? Use the pictures to help you fill in the correct names.

Hokšíla kiŋ _____James_____ ečíyapi.   Wíŋyaŋ kiŋ _____ ečíyapi.

Wičháša kiŋ _____ ečíyapi   Winúȟčala kiŋ _____ ečíyapi.

Kȟoškálaka kiŋ _____ ečíyapi.   Wikȟóškalaka kiŋ _____ ečíyapi.

Wičháȟčala kiŋ _____ ečíyapi.   Wičhíŋčala kiŋ _____ ečíyapi.

5 Who says what? Match the pictures with the statements.

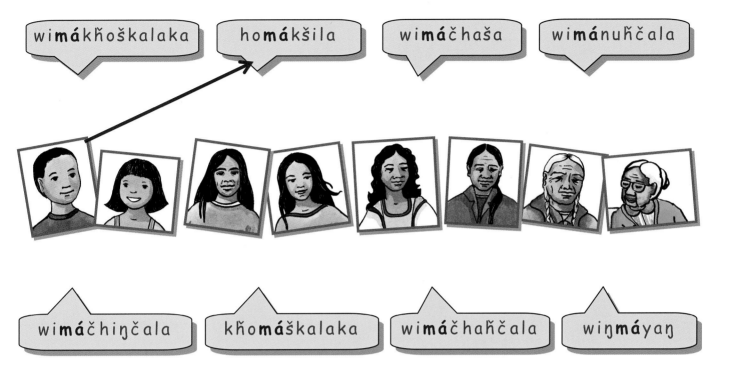

| wimákȟoškalaka | homákšila | wimáčhaša | wimánuȟčala |

| wimáčhiŋčala | kȟomáškalaka | wimáčhaȟčala | wiŋmáyaŋ |

6 Another way to say 'I am a boy' is Hokšíla hemáčha.
Homákšila. = Hokšíla **hemáčha.**
Match the other sentences that mean the same.

Homákšila.	Wičháša hemáčha.	**I am** a girl.
Wimáčhiŋčala.	Hokšíla hemáčha.	**I am** a man.
Wimáčhaȟčala.	Wičhíŋčala hemáčha.	**I am** a woman.
Wimáčhaša.	Winúȟčala hemáčha.	**I am** a boy.
Wiŋmáyaŋ.	Wičháȟčala hemáčha.	**I am** a young woman.
Wimákȟoškalaka.	Wíŋyaŋ hemáčha.	**I am** a young man.
Kȟomáškalaka.	Kȟoškálaka hemáčha.	**I am** an old man.
Wimánuȟčala.	Wikȟóškalaka hemáčha.	**I am** an old woman.

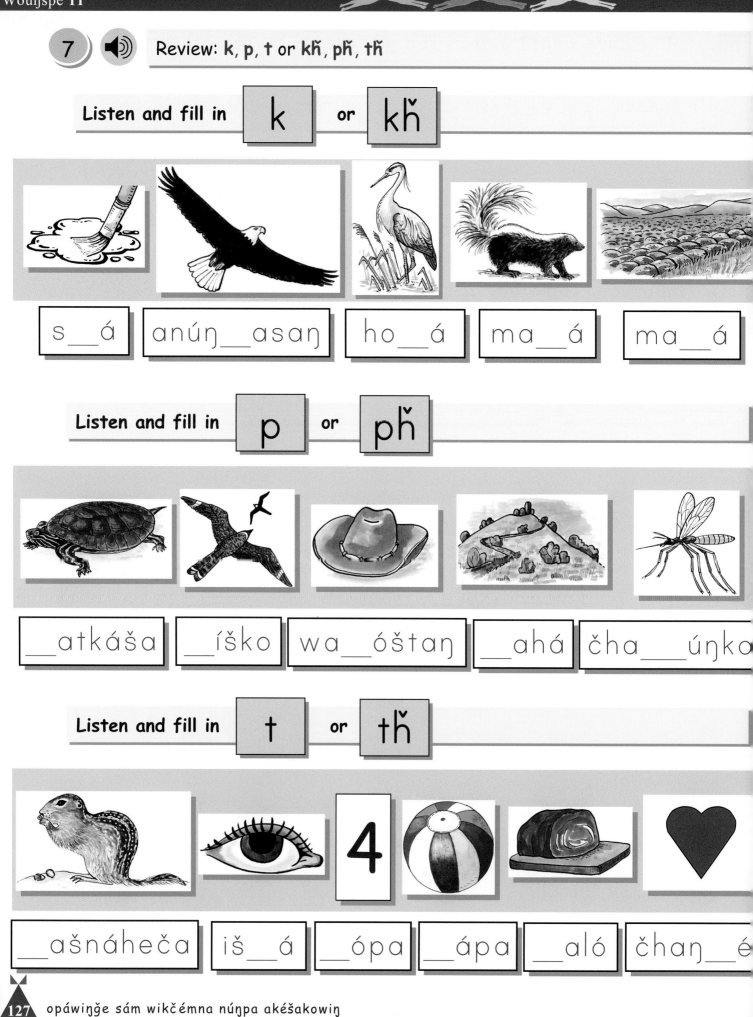

7 Review: k, p, t or kȟ, pȟ, tȟ

Listen and fill in k or kȟ

s__á anúŋ__asaŋ ho__á ma__á ma__á

Listen and fill in p or pȟ

__atkáša __íško wa__óštaŋ __ahá čha__úŋko

Listen and fill in t or tȟ

__ašnáheča iš__á __ópa __ápa __aló čhaŋ__é

8 Can you find all the words for people from this unit?

a	w	i	čh	á	ȟ	č	a	l	a	w	o
i	w	íŋ	w	i	n	ú	ȟ	č	a	l	a
h	n	a	i	ž	i	ǧ	áŋ	k	s	ú	h
w	o	a	kȟ	o	š	k	á	l	a	k	a
i	n	k	ó	áŋ	čh	á	ž	w	tȟ	á	w
čh	áŋ	t	š	a	h	í	l	tȟ	íŋ	s	a
íŋ	kȟ	áŋ	k	í	p	e	ž	áŋ	h	y	kh
č	o	n	a	š	l	u	ž	k	m	i	aŋ
a	s	i	l	á	k	a	o	a	a	n	a
l	i	pȟ	a	tȟ	é	č	a	k	iŋ	ú	m
a	w	a	k	áŋ	k	iŋ	k	iŋ	ȟ	e	l
n	a	ž	a	w	i	čh	á	š	a	g	m
úŋ	k	á	h	o	k	š	ú	pȟ	a	s	é

9 Odd one out! Cross out the word that does not belong in each line.

wičháša	~~pispíza~~	wičhíŋčala	kȟoškálaka
hokšíla	wičháša	wičháȟčala	wíŋyaŋ
wikčémna	núŋpa	winúȟčala	šakówiŋ
wakáŋ kiŋ	tȟéča kiŋ	wakȟáŋheža	oákaŋke
maká	waŋblí	tȟatȟáŋka	tópa
tȟáŋka kiŋ	záptaŋ	šaglóǧaŋ	šakówiŋ
tȟózi	zíša	wičháȟčala	tȟóša
wičhíŋčala	tȟaspáŋ	zíškopa	wagmúšpaŋšni
akáŋwowapi	čhaŋbláska	wíčazo	wičháša
hokšíla	wičhíŋčala	wikȟóškalaka	wíŋyaŋ

10 Match the words for people with their stages of life.

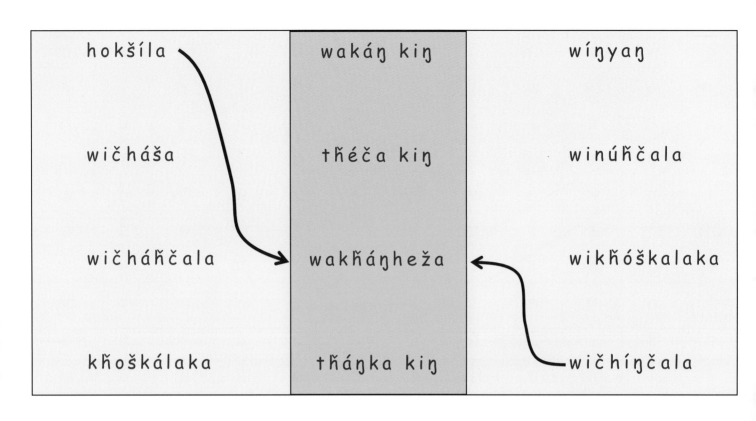

hokšíla

wicháša

wičháȟčala

kȟoškálaka

wakáŋ kiŋ

tȟéča kiŋ

wakȟáŋheža

tȟáŋka kiŋ

wíŋyaŋ

winúȟčala

wikȟóškalaka

wičhíŋčala

11 Connect the words with the picture that matches.

wičhíŋčala

wikȟóškalaka

hokšíla

kȟoškálaka

winúȟčala

wičháša

wičháȟčala

wíŋyaŋ

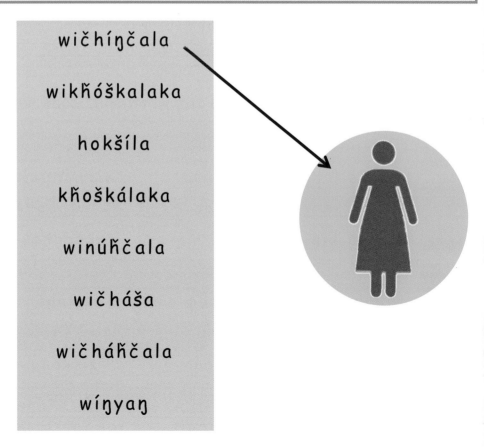

12 🔊 Review: **k, p, t** or **kh, ph, th.**

Listen and fill in [**k**] or [**kh**]

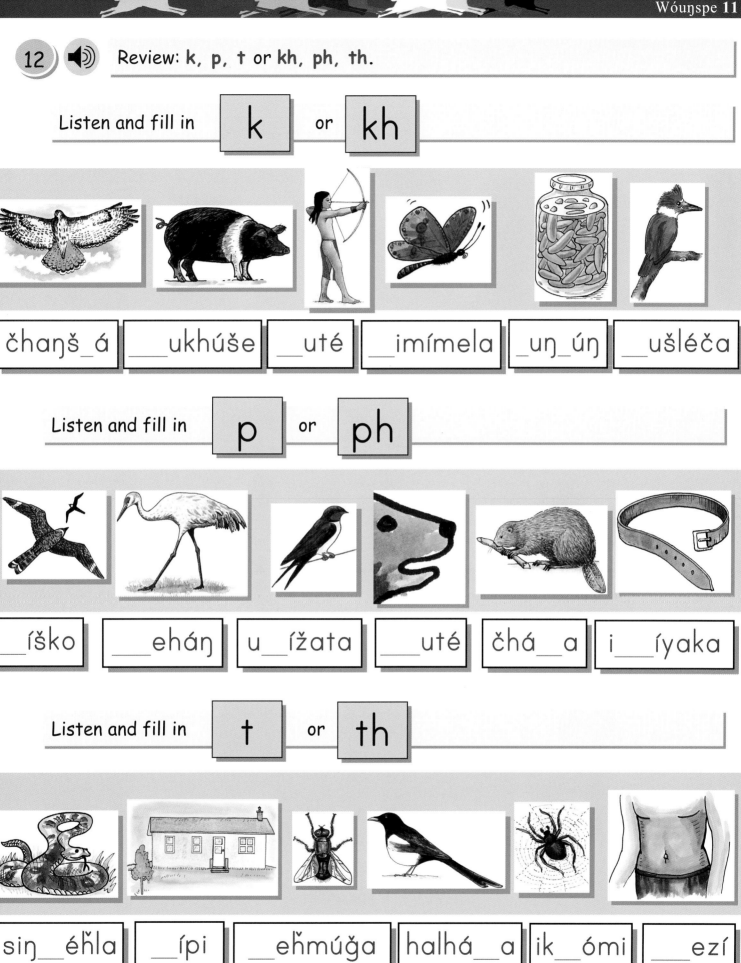

| čhaŋš_á | __ukhúše | __uté | __imímela | _uŋ_úŋ | __ušléča |

Listen and fill in [**p**] or [**ph**]

| _íško | __eháŋ | u__ížata | __uté | čhá_a | i__íyaka |

Listen and fill in [**t**] or [**th**]

| siŋ__éȟla | __ípi | __eȟmúǧa | halhá_a | ik_ómi | __ezí |

13 | **Nitáku na nitúwe hwo/he?   What and who are you?**

Hé **táku** he?

Hé **Lakȟóta hokšíla** héčha.

Hé **tuwé** he?

Hé Martin é.

Martin

Read Bob and Lisa's dialog. Can you guess what they are saying?
Based on their dialog fill in táku or tuwé below:

Lé _____ he?   Lé **wičhíŋčala** héčha.

Lé _____ he?   Lé **Lucy** é.

Fill in héčha or é below:

Lé táku he?   Lé **wičháša** _____ .

Lé tuwé he?   Lé **Alex** _____ .

When do we use **táku** and when **tuwé**?
Lé táku he? = What is he/she? (It is used when asking about tribe,
nationality, stage of life, occupation).
Lé tuwé he? = Who is he/she? (Used when asking about someone's name or
their relationship to someone; 'He is Robert', 'He is Peter's brother' etc.)

14　What and who are they? Can you answer the questions?

Anita emáčiyapi.

Lé **táku** hwo/he?　Lé ___winyaŋ___ héčha.

Lé **tuwé** hwo/he?　Lé ___Anita___ é.

Brian emáčiyapi.

Lé **táku** hwo/he?　Lé _____ héčha.

Lé **tuwé** hwo/he?　Lé _____ é.

Ann emáčiyapi.

Lé **táku** hwo/he?　Lé _____ héčha.

Lé **tuwé** hwo/he?　Lé _____ é.

Matthew emáčiyapi.

Lé **táku** hwo/he? Lé _____ héčha.

Lé **tuwé** hwo/he? Lé _____ é.

Sylvia emáčiyapi.

Lé **táku** hwo/he?　Lé _____ héčha.

Lé **tuwé** hwo/he?　Lé _____ é.

Pete emáčiyapi.

Lé **táku** hwo/he?　Lé _____ héčha.

Lé **tuwé** hwo/he?　Lé _____ é.

12 Táku yéksuya hwo/he? What do you remember?

1 Read what everyone says. Find out their names, where they live, what they like and what animal they have.

Háu, Ben emáčiyapi. Wazí Aháŋhaŋ él wathí. Waníyetu matópa. Šúŋkawakȟáŋ waštéwalake. Šúŋkawakȟáŋ mitȟáwa kiŋ zí. Tȟaspáŋ waštéwalake.

Háu, John emáčiyapi. Sičháŋǧu Oyáŋke hemátaŋhaŋ, Mission él wathí. Waníyetu akémašakowiŋ. Šúŋka mitȟáwa kiŋ sápe. Zíškopa waštéwalake.

Háŋ, Sylvia emáčiyapi. Wakpá Wašté hemátaŋhaŋ. Čhaŋpȟá Wakpá él wathí. Thípi mitȟáwa kiŋ šásaŋ. Asáŋpi waštéwalake.

Háu, Alex emáčiyapi. Wakpá Wašté hemátaŋhaŋ. Waŋblí Pahá él wathí. Šúŋkawakȟáŋ mitȟáwa kiŋ ǧí. Kȟáŋta waštéwalake.

Háŋ, Lucy emáčiyapi. Íŋyaŋ Woslál Háŋ hemátaŋhaŋ. Čhúŋkaške él wathí. Igmú mitȟáwa kiŋ ȟóta. Čhaŋpȟá waštéwalake.

Háu, Peter emáčiyapi. Wazí Aháŋhaŋ hemátaŋhaŋ. Mnilúzahe Otȟúŋwahe él wathí. Šúŋka mitȟáwa kiŋ ǧí. Bló waštéwalake.

Háŋ, Vivian emáčiyapi. Wakpá Wašté hemátaŋhaŋ. Waŋblí Pahá él wathí. Thípi mitȟáwa kiŋ zí. Wóžapi waštéwalake.

Háŋ, Shawna emáčiyapi. Sičháŋǧu Oyáŋke hemátaŋhaŋ. Mission él wathí. Igmú mitȟáwa kiŋ ǧí. Wagmíza waštéwalake.

2 Use the previous page to help you fill in the missing words. Then draw a line to the picture of their animal and their favorite food.

Wínyaŋ kiŋ _____ ečíyapi.
Thípi tȟáwa kiŋ _____ .
_____ waštélake.

Wikȟóškalaka kiŋ _____ ečíyapi.
Igmú tȟáwa kiŋ _____.
_____ waštélake

Hokšíla kiŋ _____Ben_____ ečíyapi.
Šúŋkawakȟáŋ tȟáwa kiŋ ___zí___.
_____Tȟaspáŋ_____ waštélake.

Winúȟčala kiŋ _____ ečíyapi.
Thípi tȟáwa kiŋ _____.
_____ waštélake.

Wičháȟčala kiŋ _____ ečíyapi.
Šúŋka tȟáwa kiŋ _____.
_____ waštélake.

Wičháša kiŋ _____ ečíyapi.
Šúŋkawakȟáŋ tȟáwa kiŋ _____.
_____ waštélake.

Kȟoškálaka kiŋ _____ ečíyapi.
Šúŋka tȟáwa kiŋ _____.
_____ waštélake.

Wičhíŋčala kiŋ _____ ečíyapi.
Igmú tȟáwa kiŋ _____.
_____ waštélake.

3 Fill in all the missing letters without hearing the words. Hint: each one of the 37 letters of the Lakota alphabet is used only once.

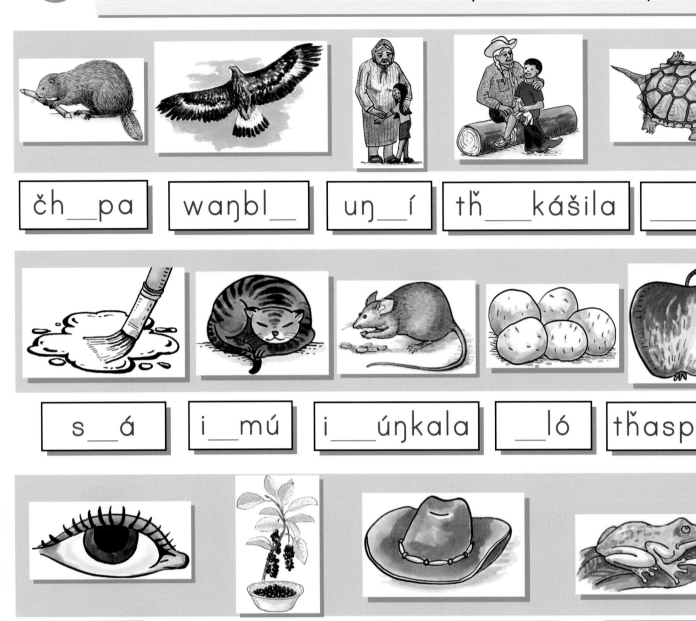

čh__pa   waŋbl__   uŋ__í   tȟ__kášila   __éya

s__á   i__mú   i__úŋkala   __ló   tȟasp__

iš__á   __aŋpȟá   wa__óštaŋ   g__ašká

pȟas__   uŋ__óǧe   matȟ__   wíŋ__aŋ   __áŋpa

Continue filling in the missing letters.

10

| _ikčémna | i___íyaka | šúŋkawa__áŋ | hok_íla |

  8

| našt__ska | he_áka | šag_óǧaŋ | iktó__i | a_áŋpi |

  1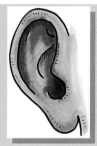

| __iyópa | ȟ_ | waŋ_í | núŋ__e | na__é |

| ___ó | ___á | ___á | ___ó |

4 Use the pictures to help you fill in the words for the person and activity.

_____ kiŋ lé _____.

_____ kiŋ lé _____.

__Hokšíla__ kiŋ lé __nuŋwé__.

_____ kiŋ lé _____.

_____ kiŋ lé _____.

_____ kiŋ lé _____.

_____ kiŋ lé _____.

_____ kiŋ lé _____.

5 Use the pictures above to help you to complete each sentence.
Tuwá nuŋwáŋ he? – Hokšíla kiŋ nuŋwé.

Tuwá nuŋwáŋ he?	_____Hokšíla_____ kiŋ nuŋwé.
Tuwá nážiŋ he?	_____ kiŋ nážiŋ.
Tuwá ištíŋma he?	_____ kiŋ ištíŋme.
Tuwá íŋyaŋka he?	_____ kiŋ íŋyaŋke.
Tuwá máni he?	_____ kiŋ máni.
Tuwá psíča he?	_____ kiŋ psíče.
Tuwá yaŋká he?	_____ kiŋ yaŋké.
Tuwá yuŋká he?	_____ kiŋ yuŋké.

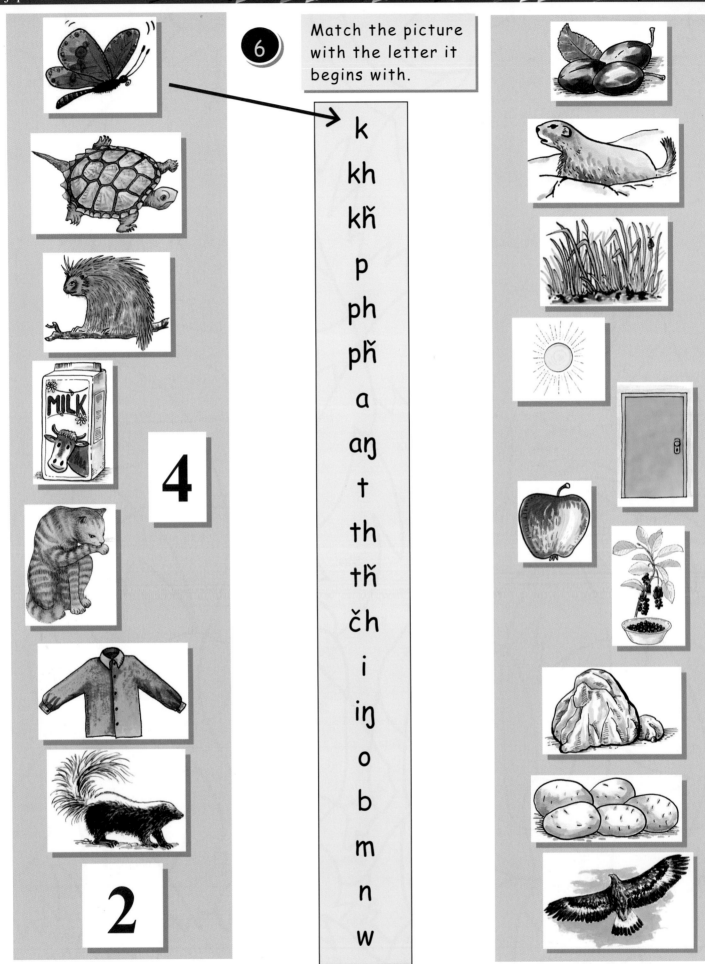

6 Match the picture with the letter it begins with.

k
kh
kȟ
p
ph
pȟ
a
aŋ
t
th
tȟ
čh
i
iŋ
o
b
m
n
w

4

2

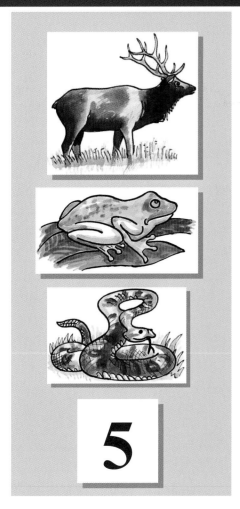

h
ȟ
g
ǧ
s
š
z
ž

5

7 Match the things and animals with their usual color or colors.

zíškopa	zíša	aŋpáwi
gnašká	zí	hí
tȟaspáŋzi	sáŋ	čheží
matȟó	tȟózi	wagmúšpaŋšni
maká	ská	thíŋpsiŋla
asáŋpi	šásaŋ	wagmíza
aǧúyapi	sápa	kȟaŋǧí
itȟúŋkala	ǧí	bló
khukhúše	šá	ȟoká
pispíza	ȟóta	

8

Animal names often have color in them too. Find and underline the color in each animal name. Explain why you think it is there.

anúŋkȟasaŋ	šuŋzíča
bald eagle	northern flicker

wábloša	itóptasapa
red winged blackbird	ferret

wábloska	šuŋǧíla
lark bunting	fox

pȟatkáša	ziŋtkátȟo
western painted turtle	mountain bluebird

niǧésaŋla (ikpísaŋla)	ikhúsaŋla
antelope	mink

maštíŋska	siŋtésapela
rabbit	blacktailed deer

itȟúŋkasaŋ	wáŋtȟo
weasel	blue racer

9 Count the animals in each picture and complete the list below.

Wamákȟaškaŋ kiŋ lená waŋwíčhablake: (I can see these animals:)

PICTURE A	PICTURE B
šúŋka *núŋpa*	šúŋka *waŋžíla*
pispíza	pispíza
igmú	igmú
ziŋtkála	ziŋtkála
šúŋkawakȟáŋ	šúŋkawakȟáŋ
maštíŋska	maštíŋska
kimímela	kimímela
pispíza	pispíza

10 Match the Lakota name of each oyáŋke with the map.
Then match the seven Lakota tribes with their oyáŋke.

Íŋyaŋ Woslál Háŋ

Wakpá Wašté

Wazí Aháŋhaŋ

Sičháŋǧu Oyáŋke

Khúl Wičháša Oyáŋke

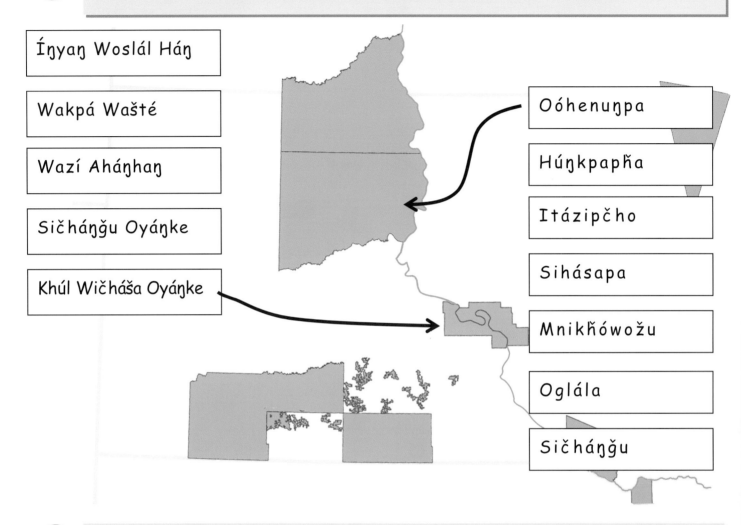

Oóhenuŋpa

Húŋkpapȟa

Itázipčho

Sihásapa

Mnikȟówožu

Oglála

Sičháŋǧu

11 Odd one out! Cross out the word that does not belong in each line.

winúȟčala	~~waŋblí~~	wičhíŋčala	wičháȟčala
hokšíla	wičháša	wičháȟčala	wíŋyaŋ
tȟuŋkášila	uŋčí	wikȟóškalaka	iná
tȟaŋkší	čhuwé	tȟaŋké	tȟuŋkášila
iphíyake	čhuwígnaka	tȟósapa	wapȟóštaŋ
thibló	čhuwé	iná	maká
hokšíla	tȟaspáŋzi	wagmíza	tȟaló
misúŋkala	čhiyé	thibló	até
ištá	ištíŋma	nážiŋ	psíča
hokšíla	wičhíŋčala	wikȟóškalaka	wíŋyaŋ
wakáŋ kiŋ	tȟéča kiŋ	wakȟáŋheža	wíčazo
ištá	thezí	čhuwígnaka	čhuwí
até	iná	uŋčí	mitȟáŋkala

12 True or false? Circle **Háŋ** or **Hiyá**. Use the pictures to help you decide if the sentences below are true or false.

Wóžapi waštéwalake šni.

Waníyetu mašákpe.

Tom emáčiyapi.

Cherry Creek él wathí.

Vivian emáčiyapi.

Kȟáŋta waštéwalake.

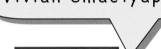

Šúŋkawakȟáŋ kiŋ hé zí.	Háŋ	Hiyá	Hokšíla kiŋ hé wapȟóštaŋ tȟáwa kiŋ šá.	Háŋ	Hiyá
Wičhíŋčala kiŋ hé máni.	Háŋ	Hiyá	Wičháȟčala kiŋ hé uŋzóǧe tȟáwa tȟó.	Háŋ	Hiyá
Šúŋkawakȟáŋ kiŋ hé íŋyaŋke.	Háŋ	Hiyá	Wičháša kiŋ hé kȟáŋta waštélake.	Háŋ	Hiyá
Wičháȟčala kiŋ hé ištíŋme.	Háŋ	Hiyá	Wičhíŋčala kiŋ hé waníyetu šakówiŋ.	Háŋ	Hiyá
Igmú kiŋ hé yaŋké.	Háŋ	Hiyá	Winúȟčala kiŋ hé Eagle Butte él thí.	Háŋ	Hiyá
Hokšíla kiŋ hé Tyron ečíyapi.	Háŋ	Hiyá	Wičháȟčala kiŋ wóžapi waštélake.	Háŋ	Hiyá
Hokšíla kiŋ hé nážiŋ.	Háŋ	Hiyá	Wičhíŋčala kiŋ čhuwígnaka tȟáwa kiŋ zí.	Háŋ	Hiyá
Igmú kiŋ hé ȟóte.	Háŋ	Hiyá	Wičháša kiŋ hé pȟehíŋ sapsápe.	Háŋ	Hiyá
Wíŋyaŋ kiŋ hé Vivian ečíyapi.	Háŋ	Hiyá	Winúȟčala kiŋ hé pȟehíŋ saŋsáŋ.	Háŋ	Hiyá

Teacher's Guide

Teaching a language is a specialized undertaking that requires resources, ingenuity, and devotion. The Level 2 Lakota language textbook can be a very important tool in your effort to teach Lakota. This Teacher's Guide aims to impart many of the fundamentals of language instruction. And while no book or guide can replace experience, workshops, and a natural teaching ability, a careful reading of this Teacher's Guide section and applying the instructional techniques described within, can go a long way in providing effective and successful teaching habits. Your students will honor and remember you for it.

Language Teaching Tips

Young children are usually very eager and highly motivated learners. Teaching them can therefore be very rewarding. However, many teachers find it also very demanding. When teaching elementary school students, try to keep patient, maintain a well-balanced class and motivate properly. Some basic advice when working with elementary school students is:

- Be patient. Children naturally do certain things more slowly.
- Create an atmosphere of trust in your classroom. Encourage the students to learn and allow them to make errors on their way.
- Be positive. Focus on what the children do right rather than on what they do wrong.
- Do not explain grammar rules. Instead, demonstrate or have the children figure them out through contextual examples. The textbook is full of such activities.
- Don't push unwilling students to talk Lakota. Often their fear of failure comes from a lack of confidence. Inexperienced teachers sometimes misinterpret such behavior and think that the child is completely disinterested or not intelligent enough. In fact, a child acting this way calls for extra help. Teachers should devote time and patience to positively encourage such children. Show them that they can do the language learning tasks. Help them develop a positive self-image.
- Scolding or giving bad grades to elementary school children in language classes does not make them study harder. Children may end up disliking the teacher and the subject irreparably.
- Divide your instruction equally between *stirring activities* (moving around the classroom, singing, interacting or being otherwise active) and *calming activities* (coloring, drawing, writing, matching and copying). The latter help children to process concepts learned earlier and to rest between active periods.
- Divide your instruction equally between *head-up* and *head-down* activities (*head-up:* students look at the teacher, at the board or at their classmate to receive information or communicate; *head-down:* writing, listening, reading, coloring, cutting-out and similar).

- If you carefully balance these two sets of activity types, you will have a better chance of keeping the children motivated and focused on learning. They are more likely to enjoy Lakota classes and learn.
- Don't do any one activity for longer than 5–7 minutes. Exercises that involve coloring or matching can be longer. Young children are generally unable to concentrate on a single activity as long as adults do.
- Monitor the children's behavior very closely in order to determine when they are no longer able to concentrate on the given activity. If so, change to a different activity type.
- Make the children personally involved. Have them talk about their own interests and things they like and dislike. Make them feel that their personal response is welcome. It often helps if they can display their work and be praised for it.
- Use commands and other repetitive contextual sentences in Lakota. Try not to over-use Lakota in cases where the children could not guess the meaning – this could intimidate them. Don't hesitate to use English when you need to explain an activity.
- Make it clear that ridiculing another student's performance is not tolerated in your class.
- Try to avoid rewards. Most research suggests that rewards make the child focus on external awards rather than on their own feelings of success and satisfaction. In addition, by giving rewards to some students you actually punish those that are not given any. At an early stage it is extremely discouraging to be punished for not knowing something or for knowing less than others.
- Whenever possible, use language learning activities that are appropriate to the students' age and abilities. Activities that are too easy may quickly become unappealing, and those that are too difficult may discourage them.
- Don't be discouraged if you're not a fluent Lakota speaker yourself. Fundamental teaching skills form the basis for any good language program. A teacher's fluency in Lakota language at these early stages is less important than the ability to motivate and inspire the children to learn.

The ultimate goal of your teaching should be to inspire and make it possible for the children to eventually raise their own children in Lakota. Your good work is critical to making this happen.

Using the Textbook

The exercises from each unit are described in detail in this Teacher's Guide. You can always find the matching Teacher's Guide pages referenced at the beginning of each unit within the main textbook section. The page number will be in the upper right corner of the page as in:

TG: 148

This textbook is designed to review and reinforce the vocabulary and sentence structure introduced in the Level 1 textbook. This approach helps young learners achieve lasting knowledge in the language. The units in Level 2 broaden the Level 1 content through more active usage of grammar rules.

Try to use this textbook in conjunction with the Level 1 textbook. Teachers should continue to employ the TPR activities utilized in the Level 1 textbook. The Level 1 textbook emphasizes oral activities and serves to contextualize vocabulary through pictures and TPR exercises. This textbook, on the other hand, is directed towards having the students gradually grasp the written form of Lakota. The four language skills are practiced: listening – speaking – reading – writing. The main focus is on understanding and recognizing words in their spoken and written form (listening and reading). The textbook provides a large number of exercises and activities to practice and check these language skills.

Although it is important that students start speaking relatively early, it is also necessary to allow what is called the "silent period." All children learning a language need a certain period of time when they only listen to the language before they start speaking it themselves. In natural language acquisition, the length of this period varies from 2 to 3 years. In the classroom environment we have to allow the young students to go through a silent period as well. It can be done by using methods and activities that enable the students to show that they comprehend without having to speak. It enables them to feel safe and welcome in the learning process. This way they will be able to start speaking with more confidence when the time comes.

Many of the instructional exercises and activities take place outside the textbook. The "outside the textbook" activities, such as TPR, games with flashcards, interaction with student's personal involvement etc. have the biggest impact. The exercises inside the textbook are only to reinforce and supplement what happens in the classroom. They are not designed to be used as a stand-alone method of teaching. Effective instruction of Lakota requires considerable outside the textbook learning activities. This teacher's guide provides step-by-step instructions and

suggestions for both outside the book and inside the book activities. Moreover, the Lakota Language Consortium provides the teachers with additional materials for the listening/writing exercises. These can be found on **www.lakhota.org** under "Teacher Support".

Types of Exercises and Activities

All units share similar exercises and activities designed to fulfill the goals of the textbook. With very few exceptions, the exercises were designed to teach and practice Lakota vocabulary and sentences without translation to English. The teachers should avoid translation whenever possible since it is not considered an effective way of teaching.

The contents of each unit consist of:
Introducing vocabulary: each unit begins with a page or two that introduce the new vocabulary using visual context.
Vocabulary reinforcement is realized by various exercises, such as matching words with pictures, matching pictures representing words that begin with the same letter, grouping words by various criteria, crossing out words that don't belong to a group, word-finds and crosswords.
Demonstration: in this type of exercise Bob and Lisa demonstrate the activity that the students (and sometimes the teacher) should do in the classroom.
Reading and writing exercises: students learn how to read and write Lakota letters and diacritics. These exercises should always be preceded by activities involving flashcards of Lakota letters. Teachers can download printable sheets and flashcards of all Lakota letters from the Lakota Language Consortium web-site: **www.lakhota.org**. Print and distribute them to students. Students then raise the appropriate flashcard upon hearing the letter. They also connect consonants with vowels to create the Lakota syllables they hear from the teacher or from the CD.
Before the writing exercises, demonstrate that diacritics have to be written immediately after the letter they belong to is written, and not after the word is finished. Check that the students do this.
Listen and fill in the missing letter:
This type of exercise is designed to reinforce the students' recognition of Lakota sounds and allow them to practice writing the appropriate letters. The pictures keep the children interested in the exercise and also help in reinforcing the vocabulary.
If you need longer pauses between individual words in order for the students to fill in the missing sounds, pause the CD manually. Alternatively, you can read the words yourself (they are given in the Teacher's Guide).
Deducing grammar rules: from Bob and Lisa's dialog, students should be able to deduce simple grammar rules and sentence structures. The questions in the textbook give hints to the students. It is extremely IMPORTANT that the teachers let the students deduce as many rules as possible

on their own. Such an approach gives the children confidence that they can learn the language. It gives students the satisfaction of finding out something new and makes them remember what they discover longer.

Comprehension exercises serve to reinforce and practice the learned grammar rules. They also provide feedback for the students and the teacher on the quality of the students' progress.

Each exercise with an audio version is marked with the loudspeaker icon before the exercise number. 🔊

Unit 1   p. 1

Introductory motivation: Talk briefly about your oyáŋke {reservation, community, place of residence}; ask the children if they have any relatives on any other oyáŋke; ask if they know the names of the other Lakota oyáŋke; tell them they are going to learn the Lakota name of their oyáŋke and home towns. They are also going to learn how to introduce themselves and say where they are from. Inform them that all of these things are important to know. It will help them know who they are, where they come from and who are their tribal relatives. **Notice:** Unit one is rather long and teachers should take their time to go through all the exercises carefully.

Divide these motivations into sections employing them at the beginning of each class during Unit 1.

🔊 1. What are their names?   p. 1

The picture demonstrates what the teacher and the students in the classroom should do. The activity starts with the teacher introducing himself/herself as in [Mary] emáčiyapi. {My name is [Mary].} This will demonstrate both the meaning of the sentence and the activity. Teacher then asks individual students: Táku cníčiyapi hwo/he? {What is your name?}

🔊 2. Saying your name   p. 2

- Have the children look at the pictures.
- Play the two dialogs from the CD.
- Ask the children if they notice any difference in the way the boy and the girl ask, "What is your name?"
- Have the children answer the written questions and check their answers by asking other students.
- Have the students ask each other their names. You may want to have a couple of better students demonstrate.

🔊 3. Reading and writing Lakota oral vowels   p. 3

- **Outside the book:** Use flashcards with the oral vowels (on the board or in your hand). Point at **a** and play the CD (or say it). Students repeat. Do the same with the other vowels.
- "Point at what you hear!" (Say the five vowels at random, students react by pointing at the flashcard with the letter they hear).

- **Inside the book:** Students listen to vowel **a**, and practice saying and writing it. Repeat with the other vowels.
- If the children can't do all five vowels without getting bored, divide the activity into two sections with a different activity type in between.

NOTICE: make sure that you refer to Lakota vowels by their Lakota pronunciation consistently. If you refer to "e" and "i" the way they are called in English, the students will be confused. Explain that the vowels have different names in Lakota than they do in English. Additionally, you may want to do a TPR with cards of "e" and "i" only.

🔊 4. Listen and write a, e, i, o, u (oral vowels)   p. 4

- Precede this exercise with a TPR from Level 1 using a flashcard activity from Level 1 or a similar "head-up" "stirring" exercise or a "head-down" drawing activity.
- If the children can't complete the entire page at once, divide it into smaller sections with activities of a different type in between.
- Pause the CD after each letter if you feel the pauses between individual words are not long enough for the children to fill in the letter.

Answers: čháp**a**, p**i**sp**í**z**a**, ȟok**á**, mat**ú**ška, kh**é**y**a**, h**e**č**á**, tȟ**ó**, z**í**, kh**u**khúše, w**í**y**a**ka,
ištá, wábl**o**ša, **u**pížat**a**, wóž**a**pi, ph**e**ží
s**á**p**a**, pt**e**gléška, matȟ**ó**, z**i**č**á**, w**í**y**u**kse

🔊 5. Reading and writing nasal vowels   p. 5

- Precede this exercise with a TPR from Level 1, using the flashcard activity from unit 13 or a similar "head-up" "stirring" type of exercise.
- **Outside the book:** Use cards with the nasal vowels. Raise the flashcard with **aŋ** and play the CD (or say it). Students repeat. Do the same with the other vowels.
- "Point at what you hear!" (Say the five vowels at random, students react by pointing at the flashcard with the letter they hear).
- **Inside the book:** Have the children listen to the vowel **aŋ**, repeat it, then practice writing it. Repeat with the other nasal vowels one by one.

🔊 6. Listening: aŋ, iŋ, uŋ (nasal vowels)   p. 6

- Precede this exercise with a TPR from Level 1 using a flashcard activity from Level 1 or a similar "head-up", or "stirring" exercise.
- If the children can't complete the whole activity, divide it into smaller sections with activities of different types in between.
- Pause the CD if you feel the pauses between individual words are not long enough for the children to write the letter.

Answers: w**aŋ**blí, **íŋ**y**aŋ**, **uŋ**čí, čh**áŋ**
s**áŋ**, šú**ŋ**ka, itȟú**ŋ**kala, si**ŋ**téȟla
čh**aŋ**pȟá, hi**ŋ**há**ŋ**, w**aŋ**ží, pȟahí**ŋ**, hu**ŋ**yákȟu**ŋ**
wí**ŋ**y**aŋ**, **uŋ**zóǧe, šu**ŋ**gmánitu, h**áŋ**pa, si**ŋ**kpȟé

🔊 7. Lakȟóta Makȟóčhe p. 8

- Have the students look at the page and ask them if they recognize the map.
- Ask them which oyáŋke is their home and if they have relatives or friends on any of the other Lakota oyáŋke.
- Have the students listen to the CD and read the children's dialogs to find out the Lakota names of the oyáŋke.
- Ask the children to point at the oyáŋke you name in Lakota (name at random).
- Ask them to name the child that comes from the oyáŋke you name in Lakota (name at random).
- Listen again to find out what is Bob and Lisa's hometown.
- Ask the children to say where they live using constructions like [Porcupine] él wathí. {I live in [Porcupine]}.

The children should learn how to say the Lakota name of their oyáŋke and hometown and to say where they live in Lakota. This activity's goal is not to memorize the Lakota names for all the oyáŋke, this will come at a higher level.

🔊 8. Where did the itȟáŋčhaŋ settle? p. 8

A TPR or a break activity should precede this exercise.

A)

Ask the children to look at the page and tell you if they know any of the itȟáŋčhaŋ in the pictures.

- Introduce them to the English translation of the names: Tȟatȟáŋka Íyotake {Sitting Bull}, Sitȟáŋka {Big Foot}, Maȟpíya Lúta {Red Cloud}, Siŋté Gleŝká {Spotted Tail}.
- Ask the children to read the labels and listen to the CD to find out the Lakota names of the headmen.
- Then ask them to point at the headman you name in Lakota. It is not the purpose of this exercise, however, that the students memorize the headmen's Lakota names at this point. They should only recognize them.

B)

- Ask the children if they know how many Lakota tribes (or bands) there are and if they know which of them they come from, or if they have relatives in the other Lakota tribes.
- Talk about the seven Lakota tribes and where they live on the four large oyáŋke (plus some other smaller oyáŋke, such as Lower Brule).
- Have them listen to the CD and point at the tribal name they hear.
- Name the tribal names at random and have the children point at the oyáŋke which is the home of the named tribe.

Older students should memorize both the Lakota names of the seven tribes and their oyáŋke.

🔊 9. Listening: oral or nasal vowels p. 9

- This exercise is divided into three sections and reinforces the reading and writing of oral and nasal vowels.
- Focus on the proper recognition of oral and nasal vowels by the students.
- Pause the CD according to their ability to recognize the sound and write the proper letter in time.

Answers: **sáŋ**, ská, **čhápa**, **čhaŋpȟá**, **tȟaspáŋ**
pšíŋ, **sí**, siŋkpȟé, **íŋyaŋ**, **pheží**,
uŋzóǧe, **pȟasú**, **osúŋ**, **huŋyákȟuŋ**, **hú**

🔊 10. What are their names? p. 10

- Have the students listen to the six children introducing themselves.
- Play the CD again, pausing after each child, and ask the students to write the names into the speech bubbles.

11. Can you finish the sentences? p. 10

- Ask the children if they remember (from Level 1) how to say "boy" and "girl" in Lakota (hokšíla, wičhíŋčala).
- Say male and female names at random, have students react with hokšíla or wičhíŋčala accordingly.
- **Inside the book:** Explain that hokšíla kiŋ means "the boy" and wičhíŋčala kiŋ means "the girl."
- Based on the previous activity, have students fill in the names and translations in this exercise. **Answers:**
1) Ben, 2) Mary, 3) Tom, 4) Tina, 5) Lucy, 6) Brian

🔊 12. Writing the stress mark p. 11

- Explain that "stress" means that one part (syllable) of the word is pronounced with an emphasis.
- Add that in order for the students to know where the stress is, it needs to be marked with a little line above the stressed vowel. It is called the "stress mark."
- Then play the CD and have the students listen to the words with the stress on the first and the second syllable.
- Have them practice writing vowels with the stress mark.
- "Point at!" Do a TPR – put flashcards with numerals 1 and 2 on each side of the board and ask the children to point at them according to whether they hear the stress on the first or second vowel.

🔊 13. Listen and write the first vowel stress mark p. 11

Have students listen to the CD and write the stress mark on the first vowel: píško, čhápa, šúŋka, tȟáȟča, khéya

🔊 14. Listening: second vowel stress p. 11

Have students listen and write the stress mark on the second vowel: maká, hiŋháŋ, igmú, gnaŝká, matȟó

🔊 15. Listening: stress mark p. 12

- Precede this exercise with a break or a TPR activity. Do a TPR activity from Level 1-Unit 15 between the two exercises (unless a class break occurs between them).

- If the children can't concentrate for the whole activity, divide it into smaller sections with "head-up" activities in between.
- Pause the CD according to their ability to recognize the sound and write the proper letter.

Answers:

hečá, blóza, zičá, ȟoká, wábloša
tópa, pahá, wóžapi, wáta, ȟóta
wazí, kimímela, ištá, íčalu, ičábu
ógle, háŋpa, maǧá, sápa, šiná

16. Read about Tina   p. 13

The exercise is self-explanatory. Children should be able to do it on their own or with a little help from the teacher. This is a review of what they learned previously, except that the word hemátaŋhaŋ {I am from} is new. It is given contextually here and the students don't have to use it on their own.

🔊 17. Reading and writing č   p. 14

- Explain to the students that the Lakota č sounds a little harder than the English **ch** in **rich** but sounds not quite as hard as the English **j** in **jar**. Have them repeat č after you or the CD.
- Demonstrate how to mark the diacritic (the little wedge) in č.
- Have them listen to the CD, repeat the syllables with č and practice writing the letter and the diacritic.
- Make sure that students write the diacritic wedge immediately upon writing **c**, and not after they finish the following vowel!
- Have students point at (or raise cards with) the various syllables with č: ča, če, či, čo, čaŋ, čiŋ, čuŋ. This is to practice č and to reinforce the vowels.

🔊 18. Reading and writing čh   p. 14

- Explain to the students that the Lakota čh sounds like the English **ch** in **chair**.
- Have them listen to the CD and practice writing the letter and the diacritic.
- Make sure that students write the wedge immediately after they finish writing **c** and not after they write **h**.
- Have students point at (or raise cards with) the various syllables with čh: čha, čhe, čhi, čho, čhaŋ, čhiŋ, čhuŋ.

🔊 19. Which do you hear? Point!   p. 15

- Play the CD and have the children point at the syllable they hear.
- Ideally, do this outside the book. Use flashcards with č and čh to practice the syllables with č and čh. Have students point at the flashcard with the letter they hear or raise the flashcards with the correct letter.

🔊 20. Listen and write č   p. 15

- **answers**: íčalu, zičá, hečá, uŋčí, wíčazo

🔊 21. Listen and write čh   p. 15

- **answers**:
- **čh**éǧa, **čh**aŋté, **čh**aŋwápe, **čh**ápa, wičhóša

🔊 22. Listen, do you hear č or čh?   p. 15

Answers:

čhaŋpȟá, **čh**aŋkú, **čh**áŋ, wikčémna, ičábu
čháŋčheǧa, uŋkčéla, tȟáȟča, **čh**uwígnaka
waȟčá, waháčhaŋka, omníča, wakšíča
čhéya, uŋkčékiȟa, **čh**egnáke, thiíkčeya

Unit 2   p. 17

Introductory motivation: Talk with the children about animals. Ask if they know the animals of the plains. Tell them that animals played an important part in the life of Lakota people and that it is important to learn about them and to know their Lakota names.

🔊 1. Repeat the sentences   p. 17

- Lisa and Bob demonstrate the activity that is supposed to be done **"outside the book"**.
- **Inside the book:** Have the students point at the picture of animals they hear in the recording.
- Do the TPR activities with flashcards listed in the Level 1 textbook to reinforce the animal vocabulary. If the students are already familiar with the animals in this unit, use those in Level 1, units 13, 15, 23 and/or 24.

🔊 2. Ask and answer as the kids in the picture   p. 18

- **Outside the book:** Introduce the question Lé táku hwo/he? {What is this?} by demonstrating it with some animal flashcards: Lé táku hwo/he? – Lé šúŋka héčha.
- Ask the question to individual students about various animal flashcards soliciting the reply Lé _____ héčha.
- **Inside the book:** Children work in pairs and point at the animals drawn on the hide. Ask should each other "Lé táku hwo/he?" {What is this?}
- The traditional style of drawing should make children interested in the process of comparing these with the more realistic illustrations on the previous page.
- Don't mind younger students answering with a single word, saying čhápa instead of Lé čhápa héčha.

🔊 3. Lakota s sounds like the English s in sit   p. 19

- Students listen to the recording and practice writing s.
- **Outside the book:** use cards with s and the vowels to practice syllables with s. Students should connect two cards to create the syllable they hear or point at the card on the board.

🔊 4. Lakota š sounds like the English sh in share   p. 19

- Students listen to the recording and practice writing š.
- **Outside the book:** use cards with š and the vowels to practice syllables with š. Students should connect two cards to create the syllable they hear.

🔊 5. Listening: s or š   p. 20

- Display flashcards with **s** and **š** in different places.
- Play exercise 5 and ask the students to point at the one they hear (play only about half of the words).
- Have them listen to the CD again, this time filling in the missing letter in the words.

Answers:
ská, šá, asáŋpi, wábloša, wábloska
osíŋ, pšíŋ, ištá, istó, hokšíla
ŝakówiŋ, siŋtéȟla, tȟaspáŋ, khukhúše, siŋkpȟé
ȟnaška, píško, oíse yámni, wakšíča, čȟúŋšoke

🔊 6. Háŋ and hiyá ("Yes" and "no")   p. 21

- **Outside the book:** Demonstrate the usage and meaning of háŋ and hiyá. Detailed instructions on how to demonstrate the words for "yes" and "no" are in Level 1, page 13.
- **Inside the book:** Bob and Lisa demonstrate how to create a question and how to say "yes" and "no".
- Ask the students to look at Bob and Lisa and follow what they say while you play their dialog.
- Based on the dialogs and the previous demonstrations they should be able to answer the questions below.
- Use Level 1 flashcards or illustrations on pages 17 and 18 of this book. Show a flashcard or point at an animal and ask: "Lé [kimímela] héčha hwo/he?" {Is that a [butterfly]?} – The students reply with háŋ or hiyá.
- Play one of the guessing games from Level 1, page 91.

7. Repeat the dialog with your classmate   p. 21

Have students repeat Bob and Lisa's activity in pairs.

8. Answer the questions (comprehension exer.) p. 22

Self explanatory.

🔊 9. Lakota z sounds like the English z in zero   p. 23

- Students listen to the recording and practice writing **z**.
- **Outside the book:** use cards with **z** and the vowels to practice syllables with **z**. Students should connect two cards to create the syllable they hear.

🔊 10. Lakota ž sounds like the English z in azure p. 23

- Students listen to the recording and practice writing **ž**.
- **Outside the book:** use cards with **ž** and the vowels to practice syllables with **ž**. Have students connect two cards to create the syllable they hear.

🔊 11. Listening: z or ž   p. 24

- A TPR activity with flashcards should precede.
- Display flashcards with **z** and **ž** in different places.
- Play part of the exercise 11 audio and ask the students to point at the letter they hear.
- Have them listen to the CD again, this time filling in the missing letter in the words.

- **Answers:**
zí, waŋží, záptaŋ, wóžapi, wažúšteča
pheží, pispíza, maǧážu, wazí, wagmíza
upížata, tȟózi, hoyázela, zičá, tȟažúška
získopela, wóžuha, uŋzóǧe, ožáŋžaŋglepi

🔊 12. Making negative sentences   p. 25

Outside the book: demonstrate the negative sentence:

- Ask the students about a flashcard with a cat: Lé šúŋka héčha hwo/he? They reply with <u>hiyá</u> and you add: Lé šúŋka héčha <u>šni</u>. Repeat with other flashcards.
- **Inside the book:** Bob and Lisa's dialog demonstrates how to create the negative sentences.
- Play the CD, have students listen and follow in the book.
- Ask them to find out how to say "not" (šni) in Lakota and where to place it (behind héčha or at the end).

13. Read Bob and Lisa's examples   p. 25

- A) Bob and Lisa demonstrate the activity: students pick a flashcard or point at a picture of an animal and say what it is "not": Lé igmú héčha šni. {This is not a cat.}
- B) The teacher shows pictures of animals and says sentences like this: Lé igmú héčha. {This is a cat}. If the sentence is true, students say Háŋ, if it is false they say: Hiyá, lé igmú héčha šni.

14. Circle the correct sentence   p. 26

- Have students circle the correct sentence.

15. Word-find with 22 animals   p. 27

Answers can be found on www.lakhota.org

16. Which animals are big and which small?   p. 27

- **Outside the book:** It helps if this activity is done with animal-name cards first (see Level 1, p. 55), and later followed by the textbook exercise or as homework.
- Make the students feel that the decision is really up to them. Children usually base such decisions by comparing the size of an animal with themselves. Alternatively, you can make them agree that animals bigger than a dog are big, the rest are small.

17. Connect the animals that begin with…   p. 28

Answers: šúŋkawakȟáŋ-šúŋka; maštíŋska-maká-matȟó; igmú-iktómi-itȟúŋkala; tȟatȟáŋka-tȟáȟča; gnugnúška-gnaška

18. Grass or meat?   p. 28

- **Outside the book:** use word-cards with the animal names and have students match them with tȟaló or pheží cards at the board.
- **Inside the book:** Have students draw lines to tȟaló or pheží, and then color the circles red or green.

This exercise checks if the students know the vocabulary. It also reinforces additional knowledge of the natural world (what animals eat). You may also explain that some of the animals are not strictly carnivores or herbivores.

Unit 3 — p. 29

1. Listen and point at — p. 29

- TPR/flashcard activities from Level 1 (pp. 90–93) should be used to introduce or review the classroom vocabulary.
- Play the CD and have the students point at the word/picture they hear. Make sure you pause the CD to give them enough time to recognize the word.
- Do some of the Level 1 (unit 1) TPR activities with flashcards to reinforce the classroom vocabulary.
- Play the CD again and have the students point at the things in the large picture.

2. Find the halves and match them with words — p. 30

Self explanatory.

3. Listen and write k, p, and t — p. 31

Introduction: **k, p, t** (and **č**) are called **plain stops**. They are among the most common Lakota consonants and the most frequent of the four types of stops. Therefore, proper and consistent practice of their pronunciation at an early stage of learning Lakota is essential. Plain stops need special attention also because they are very rare in English and so most students are not familiar with them. It is important to teach Lakota plain stops before teaching aspirated stops, whose pronunciation is closer to English stops. A detailed explanation of teaching plain stops can be found in Level 1 on page 96. The best way to demonstrate the proper pronunciation of plain stops is to use English words where **k, p** or **t** follow **s** (skill, still, spill, skate, stake, spoon etc.) In this position the stops lack the puff of air that follows aspirated stops (most English stops are aspirated).

- Have the students listen and repeat the words and syllables recorded for this exercise.
- Have them practice writing the stops.
- Use flashcards with **k, p, t** placed in different spots of the classroom to have the children point at the one they hear in a Lakota word (read or play the words from exercise 6).

4. Listen and write k, p and t — p. 32

Answers:
K: **k**imímela, čha**ŋšká**, gna**ška**, ma**ká**
P: **p**ispíza, **p**íško, u**p**ížata, čhá**p**a
T: **t**ópa, maš**t**íŋska, ma**t**úška, ik**t**ómi

5. How many objects are there? — p. 33

This is a comprehension exercise to check and reinforce the knowledge of the classroom vocabulary. It should keep students motivated by having them count and find all the objects. Have them compare the results with their classmates. Help them decide on the proper numbers.

6. Listen and write k, p or t — p. 34

- Display flashcards with **k, p, t** in different places.
- Play the exercise 6 audio and ask the students to point at the letter of the sound they hear.
- Have them listen to the CD again, this time filling in the missing letter in the words.

Answers:
halhá**t**a, gnugnú**šk**a, ȟoká, siŋté**ȟl**a
ská, i**št**á, sá**p**a, i**šp**á, čhaŋ**k**ú
píško, šakówiŋ, istó, na**p**é, heȟáka
háŋ**p**a, pahá, kuŋ**k**úŋ, wá**t**a, čhaŋté

7. When do we say lé (this) and hé (that)? — p. 3_

- Do a demonstration of lé {this} and hé {that} with an object: First hold it in your hand or touch it and say: lé. Then step away from it and point at it saying lé. Repeat with other objects. Do the same with the whole sentence Lé/Hé wíyatke héčha.
- Bob and Lisa demonstrate the meaning and usage of lé {this} and hé {that}.
- Have the students make a rule by answering the questions at the bottom of the page.
- Hold objects or flashcards near or far from individual students and ask them to react with lé or hé (older or more skillful students can react with full sentences).

8. Write lé or hé — p. 3_

Self-explanatory.

9. Find a partner — p. 3_

- Bob and Lisa demonstrate the students' activity.

10. Find a partner — p. 3_

- The students should ideally stand in a circle during this activity using flashcards they hold in their hands.

11. Find a partner — p. 3_

Bob and Lisa demonstrate one of the guessing activities (explained also in Level 1 textbook).

12. Commands — p. 3_

- Have the students listen to the CD and follow the pictures. They should be able to guess the commands.
- Use these commands in your classes consistently.

13. Crossword — p. 3_

14. Word find — p. 4_

Answers can be found on www.lakhota.org

15. Draw a circle around the animals … — p. 4_

Self explanatory.

1. Listen and write the numbers   p. 41

- Have students listen to the CD and write the missing numbers. Then they match the words with the digits.
- Detailed instructions on teaching Lakota numbers are in Level 1, page 17.

2. Match the numbers with the things   p. 42

- Have tudents match digits with pictures and descriptions. Notice: This is the first time they are exposed to the modifier position (number follows the noun). It will be demonstrated later on and there is no need to explain it in this unit.

3. Are the numbers correct?   p. 43

Comprehension exercise.

4. How many words for numbers can you find? p. 44

Answers on www.lakhota.org

5. Commands   p. 44

Students listen to the recording and follow the pictures. Try to use these commands consistently in your classes.

6. Reading and writing h   p. 45

Write the syllables and listen to them.

7. Reading and writing ȟ   p. 45

Write the syllables and listen to them.

8. Listen and write h or ȟ   p. 46

- This activity should be preceded by a break or a TPR activity.
- Display flashcards with h and ȟ in different places.
- Play the CD and ask the students to point at the letter they hear in the words.
- Have them listen to the CD again, this time having them fill in the missing letter in the words (make sure to pause the CD if the students need more time to fill in the letter).

Answer:

hokšíla, ȟé, hoká, ȟoká, hú

háŋpa, waȟčá, hoyázela, hečá, ȟóta

haȟpíya, huŋská, wičháȟpi, hí, hiŋháŋ

waȟpé, halháta, siŋtéȟla, mahéluŋpi

9. How old are they?   p. 47

The children in the illustrations demonstrate the question-and-answer dialog for age.

- Students listen to the CD and follow the dialogs in the book. If they can't guess it, help them figure out the meaning of Waníyetu nitóna hwo/he? {How old are you?}
- Give them hints on how to write their age.

- Ask individual students: Waníyetu nitóna hwo/he? They reply in Lakota.

10. How old are they?   p. 48

A comprehension exercise to reinforce understanding and using the learned vocabulary, sentences and dialogs.

- Have the students read what the children say and fill in the number of years in the sentences below.
- When they are finished, ask the students: Mary waníyetu tóna hwo/he? – They reply Mary waníyetu šákpe. Then you can ask about the other characters or have the students ask each other about them.

11. What time is it?   p. 49

Bob and Lisa demonstrate how to ask and tell the time. Owápȟe (or oápȟe) {hour} and mázaškaŋškaŋ {clock} are equally correct.

- Have students listen to the CD and follow the dialogs in the textbook.
- Help them practice saying the new words and sentences. Have your skillful students ask each other about the time using the clocks on the following page.

12. Write the numbers in Lakota   p. 50

Second graders might need some help with this writing exercise. Older students should be able to write the numbers without a problem.

13. What is your telephone number?   p. 51

- Introduce the students to the word tákuni {nothing} for expressing the meaning of "zero". In fast speech it is pronounced tágni.
- Have students read the dialog between Tina and Lucy.
- Then they convert the phone numbers from words to figures.
- They can add their friends' or their own phone-numbers in Lakota.

14. Connect the numbers   p. 52

- Have students connect the numbers to find out what animal is hidden in the picture.

15. Can you add and subtract in Lakota?   p. 52

Self-explanatory.

16. Odd one out!   p. 52

Have students cross out the word that does not belong in each line.

Topic/vocabulary: groceries, mainly fruit and vegetables. Teachers should broaden the vocabulary in this unit by using units 10 and 12 of Level 1 textbook.

🔊 1. Lisa and Bob went grocery shopping   p. 53

- Have students listen to the CD and then match the groceries with their descriptions. They can figure out the correct match with the help of the numbers.
- Play the CD again and ask the students to point at the item they hear.

2. Can you match the pictures with the words? p. 54

- Do a flashcard-TPR activity from Level 1.
- The students should be able to match the pictures with the words based on exercise 1 and the previous TPR activity.

3. Mary likes plums   p. 54

- Have students draw and write what they like.
- Practice saying waštéwalake {I like}.
- Ask them to tell you their sentence (e.g. Tȟaspáŋ waštéwalake.)

🔊 4. What do they like?   p. 55

- Play the CD, have students listen and follow along with the dialogs in the book.
- Stimulate the students' understanding of the dialogs by eliciting questions, such as, "What do you think the boy is asking Tina?" and, "What do you think the girl is asking Brian?"
- Help students answer the questions in the box below.

5. What do you like?   p. 55

- Help the students practice saying waštéwalake {I like it.}
- Ask individual students: Táku waštéyalaka hwo/he? {What do you like?}
- Have the students ask each other in pairs.

6. Who likes what?   p. 56

A comprehension exercise.

- Have students read what the children say. Match what the children say with the pictures of food and finish the sentences below.
- Teachers should give appropriate help and check by asking as follows: Lucy táku wáštélaka hwo/he?

🔊 7. Reading and writing kȟ, pȟ, tȟ   p. 57

Intro: These are aspirated stops with guttural aspiration. They are the most frequent of the four types of Lakota stops. They occur consistently before **a, aŋ, o, uŋ** and very occasionally before **iŋ**. Also, whenever e or iŋ are the results of ablauted final a, the aspiration before them is guttural as in: epȟá {I said} => epȟé ló {I said} => epȟíŋ kte {I will say}.

Furthermore, aspiration can be either guttural or soft before the vowel e, depending on the individual speakers or local speech habits. Thus the following pairs of pronunciation can be heard: kȟéya-khéya, pȟehíŋ-phehíŋ, tȟéča-théča.
Pronunciation of **kȟ, pȟ, tȟ** is very close to the English stops, but with guttural aspiration. Students must practice these.

- Have the students listen and repeat the words and syllables recorded for this exercise, one stop at a time. Show them how to pronounce kȟ by putting together k and ȟ (both of which they learned in previous units). Have them pronounce the two letters as one sound.
- Have them practice writing the stops. Demonstrate how the students must get into the habit of always writing the diacritics above ȟ immediately and not waiting until they finish the syllable or word.
- Place the **kȟ, pȟ, tȟ** flashcards in different locations around the classroom to have the students point at the one they hear in a Lakota word (read or play the word from exercise 10 of this unit).
- Have the students point at the **kȟ, pȟ, tȟ** flashcard syllables.

Note: This type of stop occurs only in Lakota dialect and in the western Dakota dialect (Yankton-Yanktonai). In the eastern Dakota dialects (Santee-Sisseton) only the regular aspirated stops (**kh, ph, th**) are pronounced.

🔊 8. Listen and write kȟ, pȟ, and tȟ   p. 58

Answers:
kȟ: **kȟáŋta, kȟokȟóyaȟ'aŋla, kȟaŋǧí, makȟóčhe**
pȟ: **pȟahíŋ, pȟasú, čhaŋpȟá, pȟaŋǧí zizí**
tȟ: **tȟatȟáŋka, tȟápa, tȟózi, matȟó**

9. How many are there?   p. 59

- Have students count and then write the correct number next to the food words.
- They can check each other's answers or the teacher may check by asking, Zíškopela tóna he? {How many bananas are there?}

🔊 10. Listen and write kȟ, pȟ, or tȟ   p. 60

- Display flashcards with **kȟ, pȟ, tȟ** in different places.
- Play the CD and ask the students to point at the letter they hear in the words.
- Have them listen to the CD again, this time filling in the missing letter. Make sure to pause the CD if the students need more time to fill in the letter.

Answers:
Lakȟóta, wapȟóštaŋ, tȟápa, čhapȟúŋka, tȟó kȟáŋta, tȟuŋkášila, kȟaŋǧí, tȟašnáheča tȟaspáŋ, pȟatkáša, tȟáȟča, siŋkpȟé, huŋyákȟuŋ tȟaló, pȟahíŋ, tȟašíyagnuŋpa, makȟá, pȟéta

11. Who likes milk?   p. 6

- Ask the students: "What do you think Lisa is asking the children?" She is asking them: "Do you like milk?"

- Have the students read the children's answers and then circle the correct sentence below.
- Additional: Name various groceries (or show their flashcards) and ask the students to react with waštéwalake {I like it} or waštéwalake šni {I don't like it}. Do this activity at the beginning of every other class asking about other favorites (colors, animals, clothes etc). This is a good activity to create a positive mood at the beginning of a class.

12. Match... p. 62

Answers:
wagmíza-waglékšuŋ, tȟaspáŋ-tȟatȟáŋka, kȟáŋta-kȟaŋǧí, zíškopa-záptaŋ, bló-blóza, wagmúšpaŋšni-wakšíča, wažúšteča-waŋží, thíŋpsila-thiyópa, pšíŋ-pispíza, ıŋžíŋžiŋtka-uŋčí, pȟaŋǧí zizí-pȟahíŋ, tȟaspáŋzi-tȟáȟča

Unit 6 p. 63

Comments:
1) Some speakers use the word ȟóta {grey} with a changeable a, thus it becomes ȟóte in certain positions in a sentence. Other speakers do not make this change.
2) The variations for šásaŋ {pink} are šástaŋ and šamná. Šásaŋ is easy for children to remember as it is a combination of two colors.

Motivation: The natural world is very colorful. Colors are everywhere around us and make the world beautiful. Ask the children about their favorite colors. Tell them that in this unit they are going to learn how to say colors in Lakota and how to describe things with colors.

1. Repeat the colors p. 63
- Have students listen to the CD, point at the colors and repeat their Lakota names.

2. Mixing colors p. 63
Notice: Creating new colors by combining color names based on mixing real paints is very common in Lakota. Elders in the old days used this method even more frequently than is done today. Examples include získa {faded yellow}, zíšapa {dark yellow} (zí {yellow}, šápa {dirty}) and šáǧi {auburn}.
Other common variants for pink are šástaŋ and šamná.
- Play the CD with the combined colors.
- Ask the children to look at the picture and think how the Lakota terms are formed for green, purple, orange, dark blue, light blue and pink, and if they know why.
- If you can, let children experiment with mixing watercolors to find out the outcome of mixing two colors. This experience will help them remember the combined Lakota color terms.

3. Fill the puzzle with colors p. 64
- A motivating activity to reinforce the students' knowledge of color terms.

4. This is a black dog p. 65
Note: Modifiers, like color are positioned behind the noun in Lakota. This is the first time it introduced.
- **Outside the book:** Use pairs of objects that have two different colors (e.g. a yellow cup and a red cup) or flashcards of colors and animals.
- Point at one and say: Lé šúŋka sápe. {This is a black dog}, point at the other and say Lé šúŋka ská. {This is a white dog}. Continue with other pairs.
- Then ask the children to point at the objects or flashcards you name around the classroom and say e.g.: Oákaŋke tȟó {Blue chair}, Wówapi tȟózi {Green book}.
- Then do some of the Level 1 flashcard/TPR activities that reinforce color in the modifier position.
- Have the students draw an object (or an animal) on a sheet of paper and then ask the class what color it is, e.g. Lé igmú ǧí. – {This is a brown cat.}
- **Inside the book:** Bob and Lisa demonstrate the new sentence structure and the position of the color modifier.
- Students should deduce the rule match the words in the white boxes. Provide them with adequate help or with eliciting questions.
- Have students practice the rule by pointing at the pictures below and saying sentences like Lé wóžuha tȟó.
Notice: This is the first time that the students are exposed to a sentence where the verb "to be" is not specifically present but still understood Lé šúŋka sápe. {This is a black dog}.

5. Listen and repeat! p. 66
- Have students listen to the CD and repeat. These nouns have been introduced in previous units or in Level 1. The combination of hearing and seeing the pictures reinforces the knowledge of the noun-color order.
- After listening you may repeat as a reading or pointing exercise.

6. Number the sentences p. 60
- Have students use their knowledge of colors and nouns to match the written descriptions with the pictures by numbering them.

7. Reading and writing kh, ph, th p. 67
Before you start the listening exercise tell the children that **k, p** and **t** are in some cases followed by a puff of air. Take a sheet of paper, hold it at the upper margin and place it in front of your mouth. Stand sideways to the children and say the words "**kin**," "**pin**," "**till**." This demonstrates the puff of air following **k, p, t** and represented by letter **h** (as in **čh, kh, ph, th**). Ask the students to feel the puff of air by placing the palm of their hand near their mouth and saying "**kill**", "**pill**", "**till**". Then explain that in Lakota we mark this puff of air with the letter **h**. And it is called aspiration. Go to Level 1 page 97 for detailed explanation.

Notes: Aspirated stops are significantly less common than plain stops (**k, p, t**) and stops with guttural aspiration (**kȟ, pȟ, tȟ**). The soft (or glottal) aspiration occurs before these vowels: **i, iŋ, u** and sometimes **e**.

As noted above in exercise 7, unit 5, aspiration before **e** can be either soft or guttural (khéya/kȟéya, pheží/pȟeží, thezí-tȟezí). This book uses some words with aspiration before **e** because there are few nouns beginning with aspirated stops well-suited as illustrations.

🔊 8. What do you hear? Listen and point   p. 68
Have students point at the syllables they hear.

🔊 9. Listen and write kh   p. 69
khukhúše, khuté, makhú, khéya, khušléča

🔊 10. Listen and write ph   p. 69
phuté, phetížaŋžaŋ, phehâŋ, phežíȟota

🔊 11. Listen and write th   p. 69
thípi, thiíkčeya, thezí, thíŋpsila, thuswéčha

12. What color is the outcome?   p. 70

- As a review, have students color the images and write the combined colors: zíša, tȟóša, tȟósaŋ, šásaŋ, tȟósapa and tȟózi.

🔊 13. The dog is black   p. 71
Bob demonstrates the following new grammar rules:
1) The sentence, "This is a dog" can be said without héčha at the end. Both of these sentence types are correct and mean the same: Lé šúŋka. / Lé šúŋka héčha.
2) Definite article kiŋ {the} follows the word it belongs to.
3) The sentence, "The dog is black" is Šúŋka kiŋ sápe. It does not need a separate verb "to be". The verb is the color here; sápe = {it is black}.
Do not explain these rules. Demonstrate them as is done in the textbook.

- Using flashcards or real objects students should say a pair of sentences, such as: Lé wówapi. {This is a book.} – Wówapi kiŋ tȟó. {The book is blue.}
- After practicing many of these sentences, have students fill in the words in the white boxes of this section.

14. This chair is red   p. 71
This matching comprehension exercise reinforces the newly learned rules and sentence structure. It adds the pronoun lé {this} and shows that it follows kiŋ {the}.

15. The dog is NOT white   p. 72
This is a comprehension exercise to check and reinforce the newly acquired knowledge.

🔊 16. Read the two dialogs   p. 73
Have students discover the different types of questions used when either asking the color of things or the color of animals (especially those that have hair or fur).

Demonstrate this grammar rule outside the book in a way similar to Bob and Lisa. Afterwards, ask the students to react with oówa tókča or híŋ tókča when you point at flashcards of animals or things.

Provide the students with adequate help filling in the missing words in the grammar box.

17. Fur or color?   p. 74
Have students choose the proper type of question.

🔊 18. Listen and write kh, ph or th   p. 75

- Display flashcards with **kh, ph, th** in different places.
- Play the CD and ask the students to point at the letter they hear in the words.
- Have them listen to the CD again, this time filling in the missing letter in the words. Make sure to pause the CD if the students need more time to fill in the letter.

Answers:
khukhúše, phetížaŋžaŋ, makhú, thiíkčeya
pheží, thíŋpsila, kiŋyékhiyapi, khúža, phehâŋ
ikhú, thuswéčha, mas'óphiye, phuté, thezí
thípi, iphíyaka, theȟmúǧa, khéya, khušléča

19. Choose the correct sentence   p. 76
Review of lé {this} and hé {that}. Reinforcement of the new sentence structure: *noun* kiŋ lé *color*.

20. Commands   p. 76
Have the students look at the pictures as you say the commands. They should be able to guess their meaning. Use these commands in your classes consistently.

21. Can you find the differences?   p. 77
Self-explanatory. Alert the students that the words to fill in are on the next page.

22. Color the puzzle   p. 78
Self-explanatory.

23. Odd one out!   p. 78
Self-explanatory.

Unit 7   p. 79

🔊 1. Listen and point at the color you hear   p. 79

- Ask the students to listen carefully to Lisa. When they hear a word for color they should point at that color in Lisa's speech bubble.
- Have them listen again, this time paying attention to the word for clothing as well.
- Repeat with Bob's speech.
- Have the students read or repeat the words for clothing from the CD.

2. Match the words with the pictures   p. 80

- Have students match the correct colors. This reinforces the new vocabulary for clothes.
- Do TPR/flashcard activities (Level 1, page 90–93) to reinforce the clothes vocabulary.
- Additional activities with clothing vocabulary can be found in Level 1, page 32–33.

3. Lakota g   p. 81

Have students listen to the syllables and practice pronunciation and writing. Note that Lakota **g** never occurs before vowels.

4. Lakota ǧ   p. 81

Have students listen to the syllables and practice pronunciation and writing. Demonstrate the writing of the diacritic and explain that the students should write it immediately after they finish **g**.

Help the students practice pronouncing **ǧ**. Explain that it is almost the same as **ȟ**, but is a little stronger (**ǧ** is voiced, **ȟ** is voiceless).

Note that Lakota **ǧ** occurs only before vowels.

5. Listen and write g or ǧ   p. 82

- Make sure this exercise does not follow immediately after the previous one. A TPR activity should precede this exercise.
- Place the **g** and **ǧ** flashcards in separate spots.
- Play the CD and ask the students to point at the letter they hear in the words.
- Have them listen to the CD again, this time filling in the missing letter in the words. Make sure to pause the CD if the students need more time to fill in the letter.

Answers:

gnaška, ǧí, waglékšuŋ, aǧúyapi, núŋǧe ıŋzóǧe, šuŋǧíla, wagmíza, tȟašíyagnuŋpa, hoǧáŋ wáǧačhaŋ, ıgmú, čhuwígnaka, kȟaŋǧí, maǧáksıča wičhítegleǧa, maǧá, ógle, wáglotapi, čháŋčheǧa

6. Match clothes with things or animals…   p. 83

Have students match words based on the beginning letter. Note: the match for uŋzóǧe {pants} is uŋčí {grandmother} which will be introduced in the next unit. Students can easily match the pictures as "pants" is the last one to pick. While there is a specific word for "T-shirt" in Lakota (ógle-zigzíča), native speakers most often refer to it with the generic term for shirt, which is ógle.

7. Word-find   p. 84

Search for words for clothing. Answers at www.lakhota.org

8. Odd one out!   p. 84

Self explanatory.

9. True or false?   p. 84

Students circle háŋ or hiyá.

10. My shirt is yellow   p. 85

Lisa and Tom introduce new rules:
1) The Lakota word for "my" is mitȟáwa.
2) mitȟáwa follows the noun it belongs to: ógle mitȟáwa {my shirt}.
3) The sentence Ógle mitȟáwa kiŋ šá means {My shirt is red}.

Have the students practice the word mitȟáwa {my}.
Teachers demonstrate these rules and sentence structures outside the book first, using real clothes. Then they provide adequate help in filling in the missing words in this exercise.

11. Point at your things and say…   p. 86

Have students say sentences like this: Lé [ógle] mitȟáwa, {This is my [shirt]} while pointing at the mentioned pieces of clothing at the same time.

12. What color are your clothes?   p. 86

- Have students color the items and then finish the sentences with the matching color term.
- After they are finished, ask them about their things like this: Ógle nitȟáwa kiŋ oówa tókča he? => They answer: Ógle mitȟáwa kiŋ zí.
- They can also question-and-answer the same way in pairs.

13. Who is who?   p. 87

This is a comprehension exercise that reinforces new vocabulary and sentence structure. Students are seeing the word tȟáwa {his/her} for the first time, but should be able to guess it from the context.

Precede this exercise with a TPR activity (this and the following five exercises should not be done in a row but with other types of activities (TPR) between them).

14. His shirt is blue   p. 88

Precede this exercise with a TPR activity. Have students use the text of the previous exercise to find out how to say his and her (tȟáwa).

15. Paul's shirt is blue   p. 88

Precede this exercise with a TPR activity. Have students finish the sentences based on the pictures of children on the left hand page.

16. Are the following sentences true?   p. 88

Precede this exercise with a TPR activity. Students circle háŋ or hiyá based on the pictures of children on the left hand page.

17. Mary's and Lucy's clothes — p. 89

Precede this exercise with a TPR activity. This is aomprehension exercise. Have students read what the girls say and match clothes based on the color.

18. True or false? — p. 90

This first time that the word lená (plural form of lé {this}) is used. Try to have the students guess its meaning from the context.

19. Commands — p. 90

- Have the students read the commands as you say them and follow the pictures. They should be able to guess their meaning. Use these commands in your classes consistently.

Unit 8 — p. 91

Introductory motivation: Briefly talk about the importance of kinship in Lakota culture. Ask the children to tell you if they have many relatives. Tell them that in this unit they will learn how to address their relatives in Lakota. Also tell them, that in the traditional way it was customary to address relatives with kinship terms rather than personal names. By doing so, one showed his/her respect and love for their relatives. Ask the students if they know any Lakota kinship terms already. Most should know at least uŋčí, kaká/lalá and tȟuŋkášila.

1. Listen to how Bob addresses his relatives — p. 91

- Ask the students to listen carefully to Bob and decide whom he is addressing each time.
- Pause after each of Bob's greetings and ask the students to identify whom Bob is addressing; e.g. Háu [até]. => "He is greeting his [father]."
- Pause after each response to Bob and ask the students what kinship term is used: Háu [čhiŋkší]. => "Son."
- After you finish playing all the greetings, play the CD once again without pausing.
- After taking a break or doing an unrelated activity, use the CD again to work on proper pronunciation of the terms.

2. Who is who? — p. 92

Matching exercise to reinforce the kinship vocabulary.

3. Listen to how Lisa addresses her relatives — p. 93

Precede this exercise by a TPR activity or other "out-of-the-book" activity.
- Repeat the same steps as in exercise 1.

4. Who is who? — p. 94

This is a matching exercise to reinforce the kinship vocabulary. English terms are available to make sure that students understand who is represented by each picture.

5. Lakota l, m, n — p. 95

Have students listen to the syllables with l, m and n and practice their pronunciation and writing. Practice pronouncing and creating the individual syllables by using flashcards.

6. Draw members of your family... — p. 95

Have students draw their family members or family tree and write how they address their relatives using Lakota kinship terms.

7. Listen and write l, m or n — p. 96

- Have the students listen to the CD again and fill in the missing letter in the words. These letters have almost identical pronunciation in Lakota and English, so they should not be difficult for the students.

Answers:
núŋǧe, omníča, miméla, oblótȟuŋ, napíŋkpa maǧážu, waŋblí, ógle, napčíyuŋka, gnaška šiná, pȟéstola, maȟpíya, blóza, nitéhepi waglékšuŋ, mní, maǧá, íčalu, omás'apȟe

8. Who is who? — p. 97

- Have students learn the names of Bob's siblings and fill them in the speech bubbles and in the boxes saying Lé Rick é. {This is Rick}.
- Ask the male students about their brothers' and sisters' names; Čhiyéyaye kiŋ táku ečíyapi hwo/he? {What is your older brother's name?}. => Čhiyéwaye kiŋ [Jeff] ečíyapi. {My older brother's name is [Jeff]}.

9. Who is who? — p. 98

- A TPR or other outside the book activity should precede this exercise.
- Same activity as 8. Make sure you don't do the two activities in a row.
- Ask the female students about their brothers' and sisters' names: Thiblóyaye kiŋ táku ečíyapi hwo/he? {What is your older brother's name?}. => Thiblówaye kiŋ [Steve] ečíyapi. {My older brother's name is [Steve].}

10. Kinship words and their meaning — p. 99

Matching exercise.

11. Draw a line from each kinship word — p. 99

Have students decide which term is for males and which for females.

12. Matching "my" form of kinship words — p. 100

Matching exercise.

13. Which of the kinship terms ... — p. 100

Students may need some help understanding this activity. They are to match the picture of a boy with all kinship terms that boys use for their relatives. The picture of Lisa should be matched with kinship terms used by a girl (no or a girl). Some kinship terms are used by both (até, iná, huŋkášila, uŋčí, misúŋka).

14. Word-find (kinship terms)   p. 101

Answers can be found at www.lakhota.org

🔊 15. Listen and write ȟ or ǧ   p. 102

This exercise reviews and reinforces reading, writing and pronouncing ȟ and ǧ.

- Display flashcards with ȟ and ǧ in different places.
- Play the CD and ask the students to point at the letter they hear in the words.
- Have them listen to the CD again, this time filling in the missing letter in the words (make sure to pause the CD if the students need more time to fill in the letter.)

Answers:

ŋzóǧe, ȟé, heȟáka, aǧúyapi, núŋǧe
wanáȟča, hoǧáŋ, čháŋčheǧa, ȟoká, wáǧačhaŋ
uŋǧíla, maǧážu, maȟpíya, kȟaŋǧí, maǧáksiča
wičhítegleǧa, maǧá, waȟpé, wičháȟpi, čhéǧa

Unit 9   p. 103

During the work on this unit, teachers should review the vocabulary and sentences introduced in units 9 and 16 of the Level 1 textbook (pages 40 and 64).

🔊 1. Look at the picture and listen…   p. 103

Have students listen to the CD and point at the body parts in the picture. They should repeat on the second listening. Additionally, you should play "Simon Says" in Lakota and other TPR activities on body parts (several of them are described in detail on page 41 in the Level 1 textbook).

🔊 2. Look at the picture of a dog and listen   p. 104

Have students listen to the CD and point at the dog's body parts on the picture. On the second listening they repeat.

3. Compare   p. 104

Have students compare the picture of the dog with the picture of a girl to find out what the given words mean, and to identify which of the body parts are the same for humans and animals.

🔊 4. Lakota b, w, y   p. 105

Have students listen to the syllables with **b, w** and **y** and practice their pronunciation and writing. Practice pronouncing and creating the individual syllables by using flashcards.

🔊 5. Listen and write b, w, y   p. 106

Play the CD for the students to fill in **b, w** or **y**:

Answers:

wígmuŋke, bló, ičábu, oblótȟuŋ, wičhíŋčala
yámni, waŋblí, wagmíza, wičháȟpi, wíyukse
wáǧačhaŋ, wíyaka, blóza, maȟpíya, bébela
waphóštaŋ, blé, waȟpé, wíyatke, wáglotapi

6. Matching   p. 107

Have students review their knowledge of animal body parts by matching the Lakota words with the body parts of a cat.

7. Word-find (body parts)   p. 108

See answers on www.lakhota.org

🔊 8. Review of sounds. Listen and write s or š   p. 109

- Play the CD for the students and have them fill in **s** or **š**. This is a review of the two letters. **Answers:**

šuŋǧíla, siŋté, oíse yámni, pȟasú, waglékšuŋ
pȟatkáša, itȟúŋkasaŋ, huŋská, tȟašnáheča

🔊 9. Review of sounds. Listen and write z or ž   p. 109

- Play the CD for the students and have them fill in **z** or **ž**. This is a review of the two letters. **Answers:**

wazí, wóžapi, wagmíza, upížata, blóza
tȟažúška, zičá, phetížaŋžaŋ, waŋží, zuzéča

10. Matching   p. 110

Have students review their knowledge of human body parts by matching the Lakota words with the body parts of a man.

11. Body parts and clothes   p. 111

Have students match words for clothes with their pictures and the body parts they usually cover.

12. How many body parts does a dog have?   p. 112

Have students match body parts with their number.

13. How many legs?   p. 112

Have students match words for animals with the number of legs each animal has. Younger students may need some visual help with spider (iktómi), mosquito (čhapȟúŋka), ant (tȟažúška).

Unit 10   p. 113

Motivating introduction:
All creatures in nature are in constant movement or activity. Animals run, jump, graze, hunt. People eat, work, learn, play etc. We are going to learn some verbs that name activities that people and animals do.

🔊 1. Listen and see what the animals are doing   p. 113

- Play the CD and ask the students to point at the animal they hear.
- Ask the students to tell you in English what each of the animals is doing.
- Then have them listen to the CD again and try to find out how to name those activities in Lakota.
- Have them repeat the verbs.
- Have students name the appropriate animal in response to different verbs that you say.
- Have students say one of the verbs in reaction to your naming one of the animals.
- Have students do the same activity in pairs.

2. Writing verbs   p. 114

- Ask the students to complete the sentences with the verbs about the animals in exercise 1.
- Play the CD again for the children to check.

3. Look at the animals again   p. 114

This activity should not follow the previous two, but should take place after a break, at the beginning of a new class or after an "outside the book" activity.

- Introduce the students to Táku tókȟuŋ hwo/he? {What is he/she/it doing?} Point at an animal in exercise 1 and ask: Hé táku tókȟuŋ hwo/he? {What is it doing?} – Students should respond with the appropriate verbs. Repeat three or four times.
- Ask the students to repeat after you: Táku tókȟuŋ hwo/he? {What is it doing?}
- The students should then work in pairs pointing at animals and asking each other as demonstrated by Bob and Lisa.

4. Answer with háŋ or hiyá   p. 115

This is a comprehension exercise to reinforce the sentence structure and the verbs, and review šni. Have students circle the correct answer.

5. Verbs ending with final A   p. 116

Here, students are introduced to the final changeable **a** (marked with capital letter in the dictionary: A/Aŋ). They are not expected to actively use the rules of changeable a/aŋ at this stage, only to be aware of it.
They should be able to deduce that the a/aŋ changes at the end of a sentence and before šni. Other rules will be introduced in higher levels.

- To exercise the changeable a/aŋ, point at animals in exercises 1 or 4 and ask questions using appropriate verbs like this: Psíča hwo/he? Have students respond with a negative verb: Psíče šni.

6. Ask and answer about the animals   p. 116

- Students ask "yes/no" questions about the animals in exercise 4.
- If you work with skillful students encourage them to reply with full sentences: Háŋ, psíče. or Hiyá, psíče šni.

7. Ejective stops   p. 117

Although they occur in some very common words, ejective stops are the least frequent sounds in Lakota. Ejective stops are formed by a fast release of compressed air in the mouth (at the position of the stop and in the larynx at the glottis). This release of compressed air gives the characteristic "crack". Since ejective stops are not found in English, the students will need to practice pronouncing them. Students should not be pressured to fully master them at this level,

since there are very few words with ejective stops in the Level 1 and Level 2 curricula. They will be practiced further in subsequent levels.

- Ask the students to listen and repeat the four words:
č'ó (splashing sound; variants are č'oč'ó, č'oyéla);
k'á {to dig};
p'ó {fog};
t'á {to die}
- Demonstrate how the four ejective stops have an apostrophe and have students practice writing them.

8. Glottal stop   p. 118

Glottal stop occurs after **ȟ, s** and **š** and it is also a part of the ejective stops introduced in exercise 7.

- Demonstrate and explain to the students that the glottal stop is an abrupt stop of the air coming from the mouth when we talk.
- Play the CD and have the students point at the letter they hear. Alternatively, use flashcards placed around the classroom or have the students make their own little flashcards with the letters and show the appropriate one upon hearing.

There are very few Lakota nouns with ejective stops and the glottal stop well-suited for illustration. **Answers:**
p'é, k'ú, t'á, p'ó, ȟ'áŋ
s'a, š'é, č'ó, k'íŋ, š'á
t'ečá, šič'é, yuȟ'í, yus'ó, mnič'á
t'óza, čík'ala, š'ákeča, kaȟ'ú, kap'óža

9. What are the mice doing?   p. 119

Have students finish the sentences with the proper verb using the color of each mouse's swimming suit as the key.

10. Listen and fill in č or čh (review)   p. 120

This is a review of plain **č** and aspirated **čh**.
Answers:
**čhaŋháŋpi, čhaŋkú, wikčémna, čhapȟúŋka, ičábu
čháŋčheǧa, uŋkčéla, tȟáȟča, zičá, čhaŋkpé
wanáȟča, wičhítegleǧa, hečá, omníča, wakšíča
wašíču, čhaŋté, uŋčí, uŋkčépagmigma, čháŋ**

11. Bob says "I am standing"   p. 121

This exercise introduces the students to the 1st person singular form of the learned verbs.

- Have the students listen to the CD and recognize the verbs. Have them point at the appropriate picture.
- During the second listening they should repeat the verbs.

12. The word nawážiŋ means "I stand"   p. 122

As a follow-up to the previous exercise, have students match the 1st person singular form with the 3rd person singular form of each verb.

13. Work in pairs   p. 122

Ask the students to work in pairs. One of them says a verb in 1st singular, the other acts out the appropriate verb.

Unit 11   p. 123

Motivation: Before opening their books, ask the students if they know what the four stages of life are. Tell them that they are children now, but one day they are going to grow up and have responsibility.

🔊 1. The four stages of life   p. 123

- Ask the students to look at the picture and guess what the Lakota words inside the circle mean. Have them follow the arrows beginning with Bob and Lisa (boy, girl; young man, young woman; woman, man; old woman, old man)
- Ask the students if they know what the Lakota words outside the circle mean (children, youth, adults, elders).
- Ask the students to listen to the CD to find out how to say all these words in Lakota. Have students listen, point and repeat.
- Do a Level 1 TPR activity to reinforce the vocabulary.

Cultural note: The circle shows the symbolism of the four directions. The children are associated with the west (blue or black), youth with north (red), adults with east (yellow), elders with south (white).

Vocabulary note: 1) wakȟáŋheža {children} is pronounced wakȟáŋyeža in the fast speech. The root of the word is kȟaŋhéža, an archaic word no longer in use that means "weak". However, native speakers like to associate wakȟáŋyeža with wakȟáŋ {sacred} thus stressing the importance of children in Lakota culture. The word kȟaŋhéža is still used in some of the Dakota dialects.
2) tȟéča means "young" or "new".
3) Variations of tȟáŋka kiŋ are: tȟáŋkake kiŋ, tȟáŋkake čiŋ, tȟáŋkaka. All of them are also used for "elders". The basic meaning of tȟáŋka is "big".
4) The word wakáŋ {elder} should not be confused with wakȟáŋ {sacred}. The root of wakáŋ is káŋ {old}. Several variations are in use: wakáŋka kiŋ, káŋ kiŋ, wakáŋla kiŋ, wakáŋke čiŋ. The last two are especially common in Cheyenne River Reservation. In the Dakota dialects the word wakáŋka means "old woman."
5) Three of the terms for stages of life are usually used with the definite article (kiŋ) as they are of verbal origin (to be young, to be big, to be old).

🔊 2. "I am a Lakota boy"   p. 124

- Have the students listen to the CD and guess what the dancers say.
- Then ask them to find out which part of the phrases means "I am" (the underlined and bold –ma- syllable inserted in the noun).
- Ask them to say what they are in Lakota, "I am a boy" or "I am a girl" etc.
- They can play a game in pairs. One of them says, "I am a [woman]" choosing from the eight options. The other points at the proper picture in the textbook.

- As a review of kinship terms, have the students go back to their drawings of family members and add speech bubbles to each family member saying who he or she is, "I am a Lakota elder" etc.

3. Match word for people with the pictures   p. 125

Have students match the people with their Lakota designations.

4. What are the names of the people above?   p. 125

Using the information from exercise 3, have students finish the sentences with names of the people. This exercise reinforces the new vocabulary and reviews sentence structure with kiŋ.

5. Who says what?   p. 126

As a review of exercise 2, have students match what the people say.

6. There are two ways to say "I am a boy"   p. 126

Students are introduced to an alternative way of saying, "I am a boy." Have them match the two options and the translation.

🔊 7. Review of sounds: k, p, t and kȟ, pȟ, tȟ   p. 127

Before listening, review what the students know about plain and guttural stops. The little puff of air is missing at the first type, but present at the latter. Do a TPR activity with word-cards. Have students point at the letter they hear. Then have them listen to the CD and fill in the proper letter.

Answers:

ská, anúŋkȟasaŋ, hoká, maká, makȟá
pȟatkáša, píško, wapȟóštaŋ, pahá, čhapȟúŋka
tȟašnáheča, ištá, tópa, tȟápa, tȟaló, čhaŋté

8. Word-find   p. 128

Answers on www.lolchon.org

9. Odd one out!   p. 128

Self-explanatory.

10. Match the words for people with the stages   p. 129

This exercise should be done with word-cards placed on the board first.

A game: Before the lesson, place word-cards with the four stages of life in Lakota in the four corners of the classroom. Give each student a card with one of the eight words for people. Then have the students walk around the classroom and at your signal walk quickly to the appropriate corner. Have them mingle in the room again. Then say, "Those of you who have 'boy' exchange cars with 'woman'; 'old man' exchange labels with 'young woman' etc. or "All who have female labels go to the window, those with male labels go to the board" and similar commands. The game can be played with other variations they become bored by it. It can be repeated as a review in other classes.

If you like, try similar flashcard games with other vocabulary sets, such as animals with horns versus those without, animals that eat meat and those that don't etc.

11. Matching   p. 129

Have students decide which of the words are for males and which for females.

12. Review of sounds: k, p, t and kh, ph, th   p. 130

Before listening, review what the students know about plain and aspirated stops. The little puff of air is missing at the first type, but present at the latter. Do a TPR activity with word-cards. Have students point at the letter they hear. Then have them listen to the CD and fill in the proper letter. **Answers:**

čhaŋšká, khukhúše, khuté, kimímela, kuŋkúŋ, khušléča
píško, pheháŋ, upížata, phuté, čhápa, iphíyaka
siŋtéȟila, thípi, theȟmúǧa, halháta, iktómi, thezí

13. Nitáku na nitúwe hwo/he?   p. 131

Students are introduced to two questions:

Hé táku hwo/he? {What is he/she?} This is used to ask about someone's national identity, tribal membership, stage of life or occupation. The reply uses the verb héčha {he/she is such}.

Hé tuwé hwo/he? {Who is he/she?} This is used to ask about personal identity, usually a name or relation to somebody. The reply uses the verb é {to be the one}.

These two concepts are rather complex for second graders and teachers may want to introduce and practice them one at a time. Students can play the label game again, this time asking each other Nitáku hwo/he? {What are you?} when assigned a task to find someone.

14. What and who are they?   p. 132

In this exercise, have students finish the answers to the two questions with the appropriate information. As the example shows, the first question should be replied with a word for boy, girl, man, woman etc., the second with the person's name.

Unit 12   p. 133

General review unit.

1. Read what they say…   p. 133

- Have the students quickly look at the text to see if they can find out what the people's names are. Then ask:
- Hokšíla kiŋ táku ečíyapi hwo/he? – Hokšíla kiŋ Ben ečíyapi. (and so on about the others at random).
- Ask the students if they can find out what the people like. Then ask:
- Wičháša kiŋ táku waštélaka hwo/he? – Wičháša kiŋ kȟáŋta waštélake. And so on about the others at random.
- Ask the students if they can find out where the people live. Then ask:

- Wíŋyaŋ kiŋ tuktél thí hwo/he? – Wíŋyaŋ kiŋ Wakpá Wašté él thí. And so on about the others at random.
- You should not attempt to do the whole activity at once. Divide it into sections with TPR activities in between.

2. Read what the people say…   p. 134

This exercise should not follow immediately after the previous one; TPR activities should take place between them. Have students look at the previous page again and fill in the proper information. Have them do only two or three sections at a time.

3. Review of all Lakota letters, part A   p. 135

This reviews the student's knowledge of Lakota letters. They should be familiar with these words by now. Each Lakota letter appears only once. You may want to create a handout for the children listing all of the letters. Make sure you have the children fill in only one row at a time.
Answers:

čhápa, waŋblí, uŋčí, thuŋkášila, khéya
ská, igmú, itȟúŋkala, bló, tȟaspáŋ
ištá, čhaŋphá, wapȟóštaŋ, gnaška
pȟasú, uŋzóǧe, matȟó, wíŋyaŋ, háŋpa

Review of all Lakota letters, part B   p. 135

Answers:

wikčémna, iphíyaka, šúŋkawakȟáŋ, hokšíla
maštíŋska, heȟáka, šaglóǧaŋ, iktómi, asáŋpi
thiyópa, ȟé, waŋží, núŋǧe, napé
p'ó, t'á, k'á, č'ó

4. Who is swimming?   p. 137

Review of verbs and people.

- First have the students recognize the activities depicted.
- Say the Lakota verbs and ask the students to point.
- Then say the words for people and ask students to reply with verbs. Then ask with: Tuwá íŋyaŋka hwo/he? – Kȟoškálaka kiŋ íŋyaŋke. etc.
- Have the students finish the sentences below the pictures.

5. Who does what?   p. 137

- Have the students fill in the words for people according to the pictures and sentences in exercise 4.

Color to find out the hidden picture   p. 138

6. What letter do these words begin with?   p. 139

A review of Lakota letters and some vocabulary.

7. Match the things with their usual color   p. 140

This can be done alternatively with word-cards.
Some of the things or animals can have two colors.

8. Color words in animal names   p. 141

This exercise is designed to review the color terms in a new way. Have students read the animal names and try to guess a part of the underlying meanings. The purpose of the exercise is not for them to understand and remember all the names and meanings. Notes:

anúŋкȟasaŋ: anúŋкȟa {on both sides} + sáŋ {whitish}

wáblošа: wa- {something} + abló {shoulder} + šá {red}

wábloska: wa- {something} + abló {shoulder} + ská {white}

pȟatkáša: pȟatká {perhaps refers to jugular vein} + šá {red}; the color term refers to the red marks on the turtle's shell and skin, especially on the bottom side of the shell

niğésaŋla: niğé {belly} + sáŋ {whitish} –la {diminutive}

maštíŋska: the color term ská refers to the white tail

itȟúŋkasaŋ: itȟúŋka {rodent} + sáŋ {whitish}

šuŋzíča: šúŋ {tail feathers} + zí {yellow} –ka {such}; the red form or northern flicker is called šuŋlúta, where lúta means {scarlet}

tóptasapa: ité {face} + ópta {across} + sápa {black}

šuŋğíla: šúŋka {dog} + ğí {brown} + –la {diminutive}

ziŋtkátȟo: ziŋtká {bird} + tȟó {blue}

ikhúsaŋla: ikhú {chin} + sáŋ {whitish} + –la {diminutive}

siŋtésapela: siŋté {tail} + sápa {black} + –la {diminutive}

wáŋtȟo: wáŋ {arrow} + tȟó {blue}

9. Compare the two pictures p. 142
Review of numbers and the noun-number word order.

10. Match the Lakota names of the oyáŋke p. 143
A review of Lakota names for oyáŋke and tribes.

11. Odd one out! p. 143
Vocabulary review.

13. True or false? p. 144
Comprehension exercise.

Lakota – English Glossary

ağúyapi — bread

akáŋwowapi — desk

akénuŋpa — twelve

akéwaŋži — eleven

akíčhita — policeman (in Rosebud)

anúŋкȟasaŋ — bald eagle

asáŋpi — milk

asáŋpi sutá — cheese

até — father

aŋpáwi — sun

bébela — baby

blé — lake

bló — potato

blokétu — summer

blóza — pelican

čhápa — beaver

čhapȟúŋka — mosquito

čháŋ — wood, tree

čhaŋbláska — board, blackboard

čháŋčheğa — drum

čhaŋháŋpi — sugar

čhaŋkpé — knee

čhaŋsá yuhá — policeman (in Pine Ridge)

čhaŋkú — road

čhaŋpȟá — chokecherry

Čhaŋpȟá Wakpá — Cherry Creek, SD

čhaŋšká — redtailed hawk

čhaŋté — heart

čhaŋwápe — leaf

čhéğa — pot, kettle, bucket

čhegnáke — loin cloth

čhekpá — belly-button

čhéyA — to cry

čheží — tongue

čhiyé — man's older brother

čhiŋkší — son

čhuwé — woman's older sister

čhuwí — back (of the body)

čhuwígnakA — dress

Čhúŋkaške — Fort Yates, ND

čhuŋkší — daughter

čhúŋšoke — forest

čhuŋwíyapehe — grapes, grapevine

čík'ala — small

čónala — few

č'ó — splashing sound

é — he/she is that one

ečíyapi — his/her name is

él — in

él wathí — I live in

emáčiyapi — my name is

eníčiyapi — your name is

épazo — to point at

gnaška — frog

gnugnúška — grasshopper

ğí — brown

halháta — magpie

háŋ — yes

haŋhépi wí — moon

háŋpa — shoes

haŋpíkčeka — moccasins

haŋpóšpu — doll

háŋskA — long, tall

haŋwí — moon

hayápi — clothes

hé — that

he? — question ending

hečá — turkey buzzard

héčha — it is such

heȟáka — elk

hemátaŋhaŋ — I am from

hená — those, they

hí — tooth

hiyá — no

Hiyú wo/we! — Come here!

híŋ — fur, hair

hiŋháŋ — owl

hiŋyéte — shoulder

hoğáŋ — fish

hoká — heron

hokšíla — boy

hokšípaslohe — pram

hoyázela — kingfisher

hú — leg

Húŋkpapȟa — Standing Rock Lakota tribe

huŋská — leggings

huŋyákȟuŋ — socks

hwo? — man's formal question ending

ȟé — mountain

ȟemáni — train

ȟoká — badger

ȟóta, ȟótA — grey

ȟ'áŋ — to act, to behave

í — mouth

ičábu — drum stick

íčalu — fan

ičázopi — line

igmú — cat

igmútȟaŋka — mountain lion
ihá — lip
ikhú — chin
ikhúsaŋla — mink
iktómi — spider
iná — mother
Iníla yaŋká yo/ye! — Be quiet!
iphíyakA — belt
istó — arm
išpá — elbow
ištá — eye
ištámaza — eye glasses
ištáȟehiŋ — eyebrow
ištíŋmA — to sleep
Itázipčho — No Bows (a Cheyenne River tibe)
ité — face
itȟúŋkala — mouse
itȟúŋkasaŋ — weasel
itóptasapa — ferret
itówapi — picture
iwátȟokšu — truck
Iyáya yo/ye! — Go! Leave!
iyéčhiŋkiŋyaŋke — car
iyók'iŋpa — traditional cradle
íŋyaŋ — stone
Íŋyaŋ Woslál Háŋ — Standing Rock Reservation
íŋyaŋkA — to run
kaká — grandfather (informal)
kaȟ'ú — to peel
kapȟópapi — pop, coca cola
kap'óža — light in weight
khéya — snapping turtle
khukhúše — pig
Khúl Wičháša Oyáŋke — Lower Brule Reservation
khušléča — kingfisher
khuté — to shoot
khúžA — to be sick
kȟaŋǧí — crow
kȟáŋta — plum
kȟokȟóyaȟ'aŋla — chicken
kȟoškálaka — young man
kimímela — butterfly
kiŋ — the
kiŋyékhiyapi — airplane
kištó, kštó — female gender ending
kuŋkúŋ — cucumber
k'A — to dig
k'íŋ — to carry
k'ú — to give
Lakȟóta — Lakota

lalá — grandfather (informal)
lé — this
lená — these
lowáŋ — to sing
maǧá — goose
maǧáksiča — duck
maǧážu — rain, to rain
mahéluŋpi — underwear
maȟpíya — sky, cloud
Maȟpíya Lúta — Red Cloud
maká — skunk
makhú — chest
makȟá — earth, ground, dirt
makȟóčhe — country
máni — to walk
maštíŋska — rabbit
mas'óphiye — store
matȟó — bear
matúška — crawfish
mázaškaŋškaŋ — clock, hour
miméla — circle
misúŋka — my younger brother
mitȟáŋka(la) — my younger sister (woman speaking)
mitȟáwa — my
mní — water
mnič'Á — to dig for water
Mnikȟówožu — Planters Near Water (a Cheyenne River tribe)
mniskúya — salt
nakpá — animal ears
napčíyuŋka — nine
napé — hand
napíŋkpa — gloves
napsúkaza — finger
natá — head
nawáte — temples
nážiŋ — to stand
nitéhepi — skirt
nitȟáwa — your
nitóna — how many you are
núŋǧe — human ears
núŋpa — two
nuŋwÁŋ — to swim
oákaŋke — chair
oápȟe — hour
oblótȟuŋ — square
oblótȟuŋ háŋska — rectangle
Oglála — Pine Ridge tribe
ógle — shirt
ógle šókela — jacket
ógle zigzíča — sweater
oíse yámni — triangle

omás'apȟe — telephone
omníča — bean
Oóhenuŋpa — Two Kettles (a Cheyenne River tribe)
oówa — color; letter
oówaptaya — alphabet
osúŋ — braid
óta — many, much
otȟúŋwahe — town
Owá yo/ye! — Write! Color!
owápȟe — hour
owáyawa — school
owáyawa itȟókšu — school bus
oyáte itȟókšu — bus
oyáŋke — place of residence; reservation
ožáŋžaŋglepi — window
pahá — hill
p_heháŋ — crane
pȟeháŋ — crane
pȟeží — grass
pȟežíȟota — sage
phetížaŋžaŋ — lamp
phuté — snout
pȟahíŋ — porcupine
pȟaŋǧí zizí — carrot
pȟaȟté — forehead
pȟasú — nose
pȟatkáša — western painted turtle
pȟehíŋ — human hair
pȟéstola — diamond
pȟéta — fire
pispíza — prairie dog
píško — night hawk
psíčA — to jump
psíŋ — rice
pšíŋ — onion
ptaŋyétu — fall
ptéčela — short
ptegléška — cow, cattle
p'é — elm
p'ó — fog
sáŋ — whitish, dull white
sápA — black
sí — foot
sičháŋ — thigh
Sičháŋǧu — Rosebud tribe
Sičháŋǧu Oyáŋke — Rosebud Reservation
Sihásapa — Blackfeet (a Cheyenne River Lakota tribe)
Sitȟáŋka — Big Foot
siókaza — toe
siŋkpȟé — muskrat

siŋté — tail
Siŋté Gleíká — Spotted Tail
siŋtéȟla — rattlesnake
siŋtésapela — blacktailed deer
ská — white
s'a — as if, seemingly
šá — red
šaglóǧaŋ — eight
šakówiŋ — seven
šákpe — six
šásaŋ — pink
šástaŋ — pink
šič'é — woman's brother in law
šiná — blanket
šni — not
šuŋȟpála — puppy
šuŋǧíla — red fox
šuŋgmánitu — coyote
šúŋka — dog
šúŋkawakȟáŋ — horse
šuŋzíča — northern flicker
š'á — to shout
š'ákeča — powerful, strong
š'é — to drip
táku — what, something
tákuni — nothing
taŋyáŋ — well (matáŋyaŋ – I am
    well/fine)
cheȟmúǧa — fly
chezí — stomach, belly
chibló — woman's older brother
hiíkčeya — conical tent
hiŋpsila — turnip
hípi house, dwelling
hlyópa — door
huswéčha — dragonfly
ȟahú — neck
ȟáȟča — deer
ȟakóža — grandchild
ȟaló — meat
ȟápa — ball
ȟapȟúŋ — cheek
ȟašíyagnuŋpa — meadowlark
ȟašnáheča — ground squirrel
ȟaspáŋ — apple
ȟaspáŋ pȟéstola — pear
ȟaspáŋzi — orange (fruit)
ȟatȟáŋka — buffalo, buffalo bull
Tȟatȟáŋka Íyotake — Sitting Bull
ȟáwa — his/her
ȟažúška (tȟažúŋška) — ant
ȟaŋčháŋ — body
ȟáŋka kiŋ — adult

tȟaŋké — man's older sister
tȟaŋkší — man's younger sister
tȟéča kiŋ — youth
tȟó — blue (also green)
tȟóša — purple
tȟósaŋ — light blue
tȟósapa — dark blue
tȟózi — green
tȟuŋkášila — grandfather (formal)
tókča — how, what, what type
tókȟuŋ — to do what
Tókša akhé — See you again
tóna — how many, how much
Toníkheča he? — How are you?
Toníktuka he? — How are you?
tópa — four
Tuktél yathí hwo/he? — Where do
    you live?
tuktél — where
t'Á — to die
t'ečá — lukewarm, tepid
t'óza — dull
tuwé — who
upížata — swallow
úta — acorn
úŋ — to wear
uŋčí — grandmother
uŋkčékiȟa — magpie
uŋkčéla — cactus
uŋkčépagmigma — dung beetle
uŋzé — buttock
uŋžíŋžiŋtka — tomato
uŋzóǧe — pants
wáblošu — redwinged blackbird
wábloska — lark bunting
wačhípi — pow-wow, dance, dancing
waglékšuŋ — turkey
wáglotapi — table
wagmíza — corn
wagmúšpaŋšni — watermelon
wáǧačhaŋ — cottonwood tree
waháčhaŋka — shield
waháŋpi — soup
waȟčá — flower
waȟpé — leaf
waȟpé ikážiži — lettuce
wakáŋ kiŋ — elders, elderly
wakȟáŋheža — children
wakpá — river
wakpála — creek
Wakpá Wašté — Cheyenne River
    ('Good River')
wakšíča — bowl, plate

wamákȟaškaŋ — animal
wanáȟča — flower
wanáp'iŋ — necklace
waníčA — none, to have none
waníyetu — winter, year
Waníyetu nitóna hwo/he? — How
    old are you?
wapȟóštaŋ — hat, cap
waskúyeča — fruit
wašíču — white man
waštélakA — to like
waštéwalake — I like
waštéyalake — you like
wáta — boat
wathí — I live, I dwell
watȟótȟo — vegetables
waúŋspekhiya — teacher
wawóyuspa — policeman (in
    Standing Rock, Cheyenne River)
wazí — pine tree
Wazí Aháŋhaŋ — Pine Ridge
    Reservation
wazíškeča — strawberry
wažúšteča — strawberry
waŋblí — golden eagle
Waŋblí Pahá — Eagle Butte (town)
wáŋtȟo — blue racer
waŋží — one
wétu — spring
wíčazo — pen, pencil
wičháǧnaška — black currant
wičháȟčala — old man
wičháȟpi — star
wičháša — man
wičhíŋčala — girl
wičhítegleǧa — raccoon
wígmuŋke — rainbow
wikčémna — ten
wikȟóškalaka — young woman
winúȟčala — old woman
wítka — egg
wíyaka — feather
wíyaskabye — glue
wíyatke — cup
wíyukse — scissors
wíyuŋpi — paint
wíŋyaŋ — woman
wóuŋspe — lesson, teaching
wóuŋspe omnáye — computer
wówapi — book, writing
wówapi ská — paper
Wówapi kiŋ yuǧáŋ yo/ye! — Open
    the books.

wóyute — food
wóžapi — pudding
wóžuha — bag
yámni — three
yathí — you live, you dwell
yaŋkÁ — to sit

yeló — man's gender ending
yuŋkÁ — to lie
yus'ó — to swim as a duck
záptaŋ — five
zí — yellow
zičá — squirrel

zíša — orange (color)
zíškopa, zíškopela — banana
ziŋtkátňo — mountain bluebird
zuzéča — snake
žó — to whistle

English – Lakota

acorn — úta
act — ȟ'áŋ
adult — tȟáŋka kiŋ
airplane — kiŋyékhiyapi
alphabet — oówaptaya
animal — wamákȟaškaŋ
ant — tȟažúška (tȟažúŋška)
apple — tȟaspáŋ
arm — istó
baby — bébela
back (body) — čhuwí
badger — ȟoká
bag — wóžuha
bald eagle — anúŋkȟasaŋ
ball — tȟápa
banana — zíškopa, zíškopela
be — héčha (of that kind), é (be the one)
Be quiet! — Iníla yaŋká yo/ye!
be such — héčha
bean — omníča
bear — matȟó
beaver — čhápa
behave — ȟ'áŋ
belly — thezí
belly-button — čhekpá
belt — iphíyaka
Big Foot — Sitȟáŋka
bike — hunúŋp nagmíyaŋpi
black — sápA
blackbird — wábloša (redwinged)
blacktailed deer — siŋtésapela
blanket — šiná
blue — tȟó; tȟósaŋ (light), tȟósapa (dark)
blue (also green) — tȟó
blue racer — wáŋtȟo
board, blackboard — čhaŋbláska
boat — wáta
body — tȟáŋčháŋ
book, writing — wówapi
bowl, plate — wakšíča
boy — hokšíla
braid — osúŋ

bread — aǧúyapi
brother — čhiyé (man's older -), misúŋka (younger -), — thibló (woman's older -)
brother-in-law (woman's) — šič'é
brown — ǧí
bucket — čhéǧa
buffalo, buffalo bull — tȟatȟáŋka
bus — oyáte itȟókšu, owáyawa itȟókšu (school -)
butterfly — kimímela
buttock — uŋzé
buzzard — hečá
cactus — uŋkčéla
car — iyéčhiŋkiŋyaŋke
carrot — pȟaŋǧí zizí
carry — k'íŋ
cat — igmú
cattle — ptegléška
chair — oákaŋke
cheek — tȟapȟúŋ
cheese — asáŋpi sutá
Cherry Creek, SD — Čhaŋpȟá Wakpá
chest — makhú
Cheyenne River ('Good River') — Wakpá Wašté
Cheyenne River tribe(s) — Itázipčho (No Bows), Mnikȟówožu (Planter near the water), Oóhenuŋpa (Two Kettles), Sihásapa (Blackfeet)
chicken — kȟokȟóyaȟ'aŋla
children — wakȟáŋheža
chin — ikhú
chokecherry — čhaŋpȟá
circle — miméla
clock — mázaškaŋškaŋ
clothes — hayápi
cloud — maȟpíya
color; letter — oówa
Come here! — Hiyú wo/we!
computer — wóuŋspe omnáye
conical tent — thiíkčeya

corn — wagmíza
cottonwood tree — wáǧačhaŋ
country — makȟóčhe
cow, cattle — ptegléška
coyote — šuŋgmánitu
cradle (traditional) — iyók'iŋpa
crane — pheháŋ
crawfish — matúška
creek — wakpála
crow — kȟaŋǧí
cry — čhéyA
cucumber — kuŋkúŋ
cup — wíyatke
currant (black) — wičhágnaška
dark blue — tȟósapa
daughter — čhuŋkší
deer — tȟáȟča (generic term), siŋtésapela (blacktailed -)
desk — akáŋwowapi
diamond — pȟéstola
die — t'Á
dig — k'Á
dig for water — mnič'Á
dirt — makȟá
do what — tókȟuŋ
dog — šúŋka
doll — haŋpóšpu
door — thiyópa
dragonfly — thuswéčha
dress — čhuwígnaka
drip — š'é
drum — čháŋčheǧa
drum stick — ičábu
duck — maǧáksiča
dull — t'óza
dung beetle — uŋkčépagmigma
eagle — waŋblí (golden -), anúŋkȟasaŋ (bald -)
Eagle Butte (town) — Waŋblí Pahá
ears — núŋǧe (human -); nakpá (animal -)
earth — makȟá
egg — wítka
eight — šaglóǧaŋ

elbow — išpá
elders — wakáŋ kiŋ
eleven — akéwaŋži
elk — heȟáka
elm — p'é
eye — ištá
eye glasses — ištámaza
eyebrow — ištáȟehiŋ
face — ité
fall (season) — ptaŋyétu
fan — íčalu
father — até
feather — wíyaka
ferret — itóptasapa
few — čónala
finger — napsúkaza
fire — pȟéta
fish — hoǧáŋ
five — záptaŋ
flower — wanáȟča
flower — waȟčá
fly — theȟmúǧa
fog — p'ó
food — wóyute
foot — sí
forehead — pȟaȟté
forest — čhúŋšoke
Fort Yates, ND — Čhúŋkaške
four — tópa
frog — gnašká
fruit — waskúyeča
fur, hair — híŋ
girl — wičhíŋčala
give — k'ú
gloves — napíŋkpa
glue — wíyaskabye
Go! — Iyáya yo/ye!
golden eagle — waŋblí
goose — maǧá
grandchild — tȟakóža
grandfather (formal) — tȟuŋkášila
grandfather (informal) — kaká *(Pine Ridge and Rosebud),* lalá *(Cheyenne River and Standing Rock)*
grandmother — uŋčí
grass — pheží
grasshopper — gnugnúška
green — tȟózi
grey — ȟóta, ȟótA
ground — makȟá
ground squirrel — tȟašnáheča

hair — pȟehíŋ *(human)* , híŋ *(usually ref. to animals)*
hand — napé
hat, cap — wapȟóštaŋ
hawk — čhaŋšká *(redtailed -)*
he/she is that one — é
head — natá
heart — čhaŋté
her/his — tȟáwa
heron — hoká
hill — pahá
his/her — tȟáwa
horse — šúŋkawakȟáŋ
hour — oápȟe, owápȟe, mázaškaŋškaŋ
house — thípi
how many you are — nitóna
how many, how much — tóna
How are you? — Toníkheča hwo/he?; Toníktuka hwo/he?
How old are you? — Waníyetu nitóna hwo/he?
how, what type — tókča
I am from — hemátaŋhaŋ
I like — waštéwalake
I live in — él wathí
I live, I dwell — wathí
in — él
jacket — ógle šókela
jump — psíčA
kettle — čhéǧa
kingfisher — hoyázela, khušléča
knee — čhaŋkpé
lake — bléó
Lakota — Lakȟóta
lamp — phetížaŋžaŋ, pȟetížaŋžaŋ
lark bunting — wábloska
leaf — čhaŋwápe, waȟpé
Leave! — Iyáya yo/ye!
leg — hú
leggings — huŋská
lesson — wóuŋspe
lettuce — waȟpé ikážiži
lie — yuŋkÁ
light in weight — kap'óža
like — waštélakA
line — ičázopi
lip — ihá
loin cloth — čhegnáke
long — háŋskA
Lower Brule Reservation — Khúl Wičháša Oyáŋke
lukewarm — t'ečá

magpie — uŋkčékiȟa *(all reservations),* halháta *(southern reservations only)*
man — wičháša, wičháȟčala *(old),* kȟoškálaka *(young)*
many, much — óta
meadowlark — tȟašíyagnuŋpa
meat — tȟaló
milk — asáŋpi
mink — ikhúsaŋla
moccasins — haŋpíkčeka
moon — haŋwí, haŋhépi wí
mosquito — čhapȟúŋka
mother — iná
mountain — ȟé
mountain bluebird — ziŋtkátȟo
mountain lion — igmútȟaŋka
mouse — itȟúŋkala
mouth — í
muskrat — siŋkpȟé
my — mitȟáwa
my name is — emáčiyapi
name (his/her name is) — ečíyapi
neck — tȟahú
necklace — wanáp'iŋ
night hawk — píško
nine — napčíyuŋka
no — hiyá
none, to have none — waníčA
northern flicker — šuŋzíča
nose — pȟasú
not — šni
nothing — tákuni
old man — wičháȟčala
old woman — winúȟčala
one — waŋží
onion — pšíŋ
Open the books! — Wówapi kiŋ yuǧáŋ yo/ye!
orange (color) — zíša
orange (fruit) — tȟaspáŋzi
owl — hiŋháŋ
paint — wíyuŋpi
pants — uŋzóǧe
peel — kaȟ'ú
pelican — blóza
pen — wíčazo
pencil — wíčazo
picture — itówapi
pig — khukhúše
Pine Ridge Reservation — Wazí Aháŋhaŋ
Pine Ridge tribe — Oglála

pine tree — wazí
pink — šásaŋ, šástaŋ
plum — kȟáŋta
point at — épazo
police man — čhaŋksá yuhá *(Pine Ridge)*, akíčhita *(Rosebud)*, wawóyuspa *(north)*
porcupine — pȟahíŋ
pot — čhéǧa
potato — bló
powerful — š'ákeča
prairie dog — pispíza
pram — hokšípaslohe
pudding — wóžapi
puppy — šuŋȟpála
purple — tȟóša
question ending — he?
question ending — hwo?
rabbit — maštíŋska
raccoon — wičhítegleǧa
rain, to rain — maǧážu
rainbow — wígmuŋke
rattlesnake — siŋtéȟla
rectangle — oblótȟuŋ háŋska
red — šá
Red Cloud — Maȟpíya Lúta
red fox — šuŋǧíla
redtailed hawk — čhaŋšká
redwinged blackbird — wábloša
reservation — oyáŋke
rice — psíŋ
river — wakpá
road — čhaŋkú
Rosebud Reservation — Sičháŋǧu Oyáŋke
Rosebud tribe — Sičháŋǧu
run — íŋyaŋkA
sage — phežíȟota
salt — mniskúya
scissors — wíyukse; iyúšla
seemingly — s'a
seven — šakówiŋ
shield — waháčhaŋka
shirt — ógle
shoes — háŋpa
shoot — khuté
short — ptéčela
shoulder — hiŋyéte
shout — š'á
sick (to be) — khúžA
sing — lowáŋ
sister — čhuwé *(woman's older -)*, tȟaŋké *(man's older -)*, tȟaŋkší

(man's younger -); mitȟáŋka(la) *(woman's younger -)*
sit — yaŋkÁ
Sitting Bull — Tȟatȟáŋka Íyotake
six — šákpe
skirt — nitéhepi
skunk — maká
sky — maȟpíya
sleep — ištíŋmA
small — číkʼala
snake — zuzéča
snapping turtle — khéya
snout — phuté
socks — huŋyákȟuŋ
something — táku
son — čhiŋkší
soup — waháŋpi
spider — iktómi
splashing sound — č'ó
Spotted Tail — Siŋté Gleška
spring (season) — wétu
square — oblótȟuŋ
squirrel — zičá, tȟašnáheča *(ground)*
stand — nážiŋ
Standing Rock Reservation — Íŋyaŋ Woslál Háŋ
Standing Rock tribe — Húŋkpapȟa
star — wičháȟpi
stomach — thezí
stone — íŋyaŋ
store — mas'óphiye
strawberry — wažúšteča, wazíškeča
strong — š'ákeča
sugar — čhaŋháŋpi
summer — blokétu
sun — aŋpáwi, aŋpétu wí
swallow — upížata
swim — nuŋwÁŋ
swim as a duck — yus'ó
table — wáglotapi
tail — siŋté
tall — háŋskA
teacher — waúŋspekhiya
telephone — omás'apȟe
temples — nawáte
ten — wikčémna
that — hé
the — kiŋ
these — lená
thigh — sičháŋ
this — lé
those, they — hená
three — yámni

toe — siókaza
tomato — uŋžíŋžiŋtka
tongue — čheží
tooth — hí
town — otȟúŋwahe
train — ȟemáni
tree — čháŋ
triangle — oíse yámni
truck — iwátȟokšu
turkey — waglékšuŋ
turkey buzzard — hečá
turnip — thíŋpsila, thíŋpsiŋla
turtle — pȟatkáša *(western painted)*, khéya *(snapping)*
twelve — akénuŋpa
two — núŋpa
underwear — mahéluŋpi
vegetable — watȟótȟo
walk — máni
water — mní
watermelon — wagmúšpaŋšni
wear (to) — úŋ
weasel — itȟúŋkasaŋ
well — taŋyáŋ
western painted turtle — pȟatkáša
what — táku
What is your name? — Táku eníčiyapi hwo/he?
what type — tókča
where — tuktél
Where do you live? — Tuktél yathí hwo/he?
whistle — žó
white — ská
white man — wašíču
whitish, dull white — sáŋ
who — tuwé
window — ožáŋžaŋglepi
winter, year — waníyetu
woman — wíŋyaŋ, winúȟčala *(old)*, wikȟóškalaka *(young)*
wood — čháŋ
Write! Color! — Owá yo/ye!
yellow — zí
yes — háŋ
you like — waštéyalake
you live, you dwell — yathí
young man — kȟoškálaka
young woman — wikȟóškalaka
your — nitȟáwa
your name is — eníčiyapi
youth — tȟéča kiŋ
zero — tákuni, tágni